D1739711

Tree to Table

Cooking with Australian Olive Oil

Tree to Table

Cooking with Australian Olive Oil

Patrice Newell

Photography by Simon Griffiths

LANTERN
an imprint of
PENGUIN BOOKS

LANTERN

Published by the Penguin Group
Penguin Group (Australia)
250 Camberwell Road, Camberwell, Victoria 3124, Australia
(a division of Pearson Australia Group Pty Ltd)
Penguin Group (USA) Inc.
375 Hudson Street, New York, New York 10014, USA
Penguin Group (Canada)
90 Eglinton Avenue East, Suite 700, Toronto, Canada ON M4P 2Y3
(a division of Pearson Penguin Canada Inc.)
Penguin Books Ltd
80 Strand, London WC2R 0RL England
Penguin Ireland
25 St Stephen's Green, Dublin 2, Ireland
(a division of Penguin Books Ltd)
Penguin Books India Pvt Ltd
11 Community Centre, Panchsheel Park, New Delhi - 110 017, India
Penguin Group (NZ)
67 Apollo Drive, Rosedale, North Shore 0632, New Zealand
(a division of Pearson New Zealand Ltd)
Penguin Books (South Africa) (Pty) Ltd
24 Sturdee Avenue, Rosebank, Johannesburg 2196, South Africa

Penguin Books Ltd, Registered Offices: 80 Strand, London, WC2R 0RL, England

First published by Penguin Group (Australia), 2008

10 9 8 7 6 5 4 3 2 1

Text copyright © Patrice Newell 2008
Photographs © Simon Griffiths 2008

The moral right of the author has been asserted.

All rights reserved. Without limiting the rights under copyright reserved above, no part of this publication may be reproduced, stored in or introduced into a retrieval system, or transmitted, in any form or by any means (electronic, mechanical, photocopying, recording or otherwise), without the prior written permission of both the copyright owner and the above publisher of this book.

Cover and text design by Jo Hunt © Penguin Group (Australia)
Design coordination by Megan Baker
Cover photograph by Simon Griffiths
Typeset in Al Prosperall by Post Pre-press Group, Brisbane, Queensland
Colour reproduction by Splitting Image, Clayton, Victoria
Printed and bound in China by 1010 Printing International Limited

National Library of Australia
Cataloguing-in-Publication data:

Newell, Patrice, 1956-
    Tree to Table: Cooking with Australian Olive Oil

    1st ed.
    Includes index.
    ISBN 978 1 9209 8966 8 (hbk.).

    1. Cookery (Olive oil). 2. Olive oil - Australia. 3. Nutrition. I. Title

641. 6463

penguin.com.au

Contents

Olive. I love the fruit, the trees, the oil, even the word. You can play with it in the mind. O live. Try doing that with peanuts or canola. No wonder the olive branch is such a powerful symbol, and was, in the bird's beak, such good news for Noah.

There's nothing forbidden about the olive fruit. Indeed, the Old Testament seems to sanctify it. The oil has magic and romance as it takes its trip from the tongue's tip to the palate. O live, olive!

This book is about that magic, about that trip.

Patrice Newell, Elmswood, 2008

Olive oil: An introduction

This book was both inevitable and unlikely. Inevitable because
a day rarely passes without someone asking me about the proper
use of olive oil. Unlikely because I'd vowed never to write a food
book, let alone a cookbook. Olive oil is one of Earth's great foods.
As biblical as milk and honey, it has been part of human life
and health for millennia, central to the civilisations surrounding
the pyramids in Egypt, the Acropolis in Greece, the Alhambra
in Spain, the Roman Forum and the villas of the Etruscans.

Where other oils come and go due to fads, fashions and industrial experiments, olive oil is part of the flow of history.

It was traded long before the age of Tutankhamen. In a recent excavation in Rome, archaeologists discovered thousands of olive oil pots that had been imported from Spain. I couldn't help wondering whether there were food safety issues in that time. Did people in Pompeii and Herculaneum complain of rancidity? Did Romans sicken when the batch dates weren't correctly recorded?

Food has been at the heart of what I've been doing as a farmer since 1987, but my principal concerns have been with its production and politics. For me, recipes are as much for collecting as using. I take an ad-lib approach to cooking. And although rules are made to be broken, there's one I usually observe: my food preparation is conducted in batches of ten minutes. This applies even though I slow-cook most meals. I'll leave osso buco on the stove for two hours and stock in the oven. The food from my kitchen is easy; wherever possible I prepare things simultaneously and use up leftovers. I'll make, for example, enough stock for three different meals: osso buco, soup and risotto.

The kitchen of our nineteenth-century homestead is a place of tradition, incorporating both past and new traditions - those the family has created. It has become a sanctuary, where I feed my soul as I feed my family. Here is where my most intimate conversations take place, with Aurora, Phillip and friends and neighbours as they help me prepare food or drop in for a chat.

While cooking I look through the windows at the distant vistas of the farm, at what Dorothea Mackellar described so well as 'the beauty and the terror' of rural life and landscape. I've seen the drought biting deeply into the dry flesh of the land as the olive trees bravely struggle to survive against the odds. And seen too the rains convert the hills to green.

Now I find myself writing a book for my kitchen and, I hope, for yours. Between its covers, the politics of food will occasionally converge with the love of cooking and the aesthetics of eating. A respectful, celebratory approach to food involves a range of edible plants, animals and fungi,

creatively transformed by good cooking and thoughtful presentation. I believe each and every one of us has the responsibility to manage our kitchens and our own health. These are skills that can be learned, building on the idea that the foundation of good food is wholeness and freshness.

I want all our food to be whole. Wholeness is just as important as freshness. Whole? In other words, not refined. And olive oil, as long as it's extra virgin, is one of life's great fresh, natural, whole foods. Be very suspicious of labels like 'enriched'. Please, please, no skim milk, hydrogenated vegetable oil, protein powders, additives or colourings. And please, no low-fat anything. Beware the mumbo-jumbo of modern marketing, the jargon of deception in which factory foods are flattered as 'natural' and most foods are processed into oblivion. How could it be otherwise when food is such a mass commodity?

When I was growing up, my mother Thelma Newell would always remind me that we ate our meals in a world where others went hungry. Whilst no-one said grace in our house, every meal, every mouthful, was cause for gratitude. And food was never wasted. Our pantry was like Mother Hubbard's cupboard; our small, round-shouldered fridge was at best half-full. To over-shop and throw out food is dismissive of the love and effort that goes into good produce.

Most of my childhood friends came from migrant families - Lithuanian, Italian and Maltese. I grew up watching Mary's mama make homemade pasta while her papa made wine from grapes grown in a tiny backyard in suburban Adelaide. Lily's mama arranged all the food in the centre of the table so that everyone could help themselves (by the end of the meal there was inevitably a mess on the cloth), and in both those homes olive oil was poured onto every dish. This is a principle I commend to you.

Today, though, my pantry is absurdly crowded. Helping me unpack groceries one day, a neighbour opened the door, recoiled and said in shocked amazement, 'There's no room for anything more!' The only way she could think of to get the new items in was to 'chuck them in' as if they were cricket balls.

Throughout my life in the kitchen I've been guilty of disorderly conduct. Am I proud to say my daughter Aurora, who's learned to be a marvellous cook, continues this tradition? Yet the chaos has merit. Thanks to the abundance of the farm's produce, I'm continually jarring jams, chutneys, pesto, tapenades, sauerkraut and honey, making stock from beef bones, proving bread and drying herbs, fruit and seeds, in between farm work.

Modern resources allow me to augment the spices and herbs I grow with dozens I cannot. I grew up with only salt, pepper, mustard, mixed spice and mixed herbs. Now the pantry is as multicultural as our library. It is an act of culinary perversion that, in this era of access to the finest food in history, so many of us choose to eat processed muck - food only marginally less appalling than toxic sludge. Eating well should be part of one's self-respect. If we are what we eat, we shouldn't turn our bodies into gully traps.

The cheap vegetable oils lining the supermarket shelves are more suitable for fuelling trucks than serving at the table. As biofuels gain political support, these oils will indeed be feeding vehicles, not just people. I'm glad to say, though, that Australia's olive growers are trying hard to produce the best olive oil the world has ever tasted. That might seem like an overstatement, but believe me, it is not. What Australia has achieved with the grape, we are now achieving with the olive. While it's not the first time we've attempted to produce fine olive oil - there were pioneering efforts in the nineteenth century, the first olive trees being planted at the time of Macarthur - the Australian olive industry is currently in a renaissance. The groves of the twenty-first century mark a new beginning, although the future is by no means secure.

Thankfully, the industry no longer use convicts for cheap labour. Whilst on our farm we still love hand-picking some of our crop, we marvel at the strange, multi-fingered machines that march through our grove at harvest time. The latest harvesting and extraction technologies have made olive oil production more economical and hygienic without compromising the integrity of the product. In fact, the latest technologies help extract the very spirit of the olive.

But from beginning to end it is our soils that must nourish our trees and the oils they produce. Somehow the vast, parched and ancient soils of Australia must be encouraged to provide life and energy for our precious food. And we must learn to make better oil with less and less water. Creating olive groves and trying to defend them from drought, frost and the attacks of parrots is the endless challenge. But my friends in the renaissance and I are determined to succeed.

Since writing *The Olive Grove*, I've watched Australian producers bottle ever-better oil. Yet most people still buy cheap, dubious imported oils from Spain, Tunisia, Italy or Greece. Some of this oil meets minimum standards. Most of it doesn't. This book will explain how to choose olive oil as well as how to use it.

In the official food pyramid, olive oil is classified as a fat. Oil is a fat that is liquid at room temperature. I am an advocate of consuming all kinds of natural, unadulterated fats in the diet. Fats provide energy, and are an important component of cell membranes and hormones. They are essential for the absorption of some vitamins and antioxidants, and some fats can help avoid certain types of arthritis and stiffness. Vitamins A, D, E and K are all fat-soluble. Olive oil is predominantly a mono-unsaturated fat but, like all fats, it's actually a mixture of saturated, polyunsaturated and mono-unsaturated fatty acids. And each bottle of olive oil will have a slight variation on the mix.

I first became interested in nutrition in the early eighties while studying herbal medicine. My personal ethic is to celebrate food for its health-giving properties as well as its taste, and that includes the role fat has to play in health. Once, I confessed to an eminent food chemist that I liked fresh butter, full cream and gooey chocolate brownies; he almost froze - in his eyes I was guilty of oleaginous crime. 'But whole fats, especially high-quality dairy fats, are good for you,' I protested.

We negotiated a truce by agreeing there was merit in the best-quality fresh fats, such as cream, lard, tallow and olive oil. I eat a lot of fat. I even melt the fat when we butcher our grass-fed lamb in order to provide fresh tallow, in which I deep-fry potatoes, lamb cutlets and crumbed chicken, and every time I do it, I feel my joints are grateful.

When we started producing beef at Elmswood in 1987, saturated fat was widely believed to be a major problem. Prior to eating even a morsel of red meat, we were sternly instructed to cut off any hint of fat, ignoring the fact that saturated fats add flavour and have high nutritional value.

The carefully inculcated fear of fat has produced one of the abominations of our era - the great lie of low-fat. I see an example of this in action when a friend arrives from Sydney. She joins Aurora and me in the kitchen, and it's a classic case of too many cooks. While she approves of the ingredients we produce in our vegie garden, she ventures a suggestion for the salad: 'Can we serve the dressing on the side?' My response is a shudder. Clearly she's

a 'low-fatter'. I reluctantly serve her salad undressed, stark bollock naked, but toss the rest of the fresh leaves in the dressing I've just made.

A salad isn't really complete without a fresh clove of garlic crushed in the mortar with rock salt, without a pinch of mustard, a dollop of honey, a swish of vinegar or lemon and a generous pouring of the freshest olive oil. I'm proud of the leaves from my garden, but they need the companionship of other ingredients - most importantly, olive oil.

A week later I notice the visitor has smuggled a blasphemous bottle into the fridge, a bottle of low-fat salad dressing. I want to be understanding of my friends' dietary requirements. I am happy to oblige them by avoiding eggs, gluten or milk, by observing the niceties of vegetarian diets, by

acknowledging the pieties of the no-fish brigade. Then there are the entirely subjective 'I don't like' declarations of teenagers. But low-fat? All tolerance disappears. This means war.

I tell my friend that her salad dressing is banned from the fridge. She cannot be a guest at a biodynamic farm, surrounded by fresh olive oil, home-grown vegetables and grass-fed meat, and buy low-fat salad dressing. One of them has to go. It or her. Besides, I explain patiently, 'Olive oil won't make you fat, but a low-fat diet will make you look very old.' It went. She stayed.

Fresh olive oil has characteristics that other oils - like palm kernel, coconut, corn, safflower, peanut, soy, flaxseed, cottonseed and sesame - don't. Olive oil can be consumed straight from the bottle and enjoyed as a food, with very little accompaniment and without cooking. It blends beautifully with countless ingredients and creates infinite opportunities for combinations. Its complexity profoundly improves the diets of everyone who uses it generously. It is a virtuous indulgence.

Whether it's spring, summer, autumn or winter, it's time to soak the bruschetta in olive oil, pour it into the soup, use it to dress up your salad. Olive oil will enhance your food, your kitchen, your life.

How should
olive oil taste?

There is no one flavour. Olives are as variable as grapes, oils as varietal as wines, but regardless of variety, the time of harvest or the region, producers strive for three characteristics: fruitiness, bitterness and pungency. Get these right and you create what is known in the trade as 'harmony'. We're talking as much art as science, and as with wine, we're dealing with impassioned and subjective judgements.

Imagine a song. Imagine you're in a recording studio at the mixing console. It matters little whether you're recording rock or opera - you want the percussion, strings, brass and voices to be in balance. You want harmony. So it is with olive oil. You want a harmonic fragrance to be carried to the palate. You want the fruitiness, bitterness and pungency to be in tune.

Before you taste an oil, appreciate its aroma. As with tasting wine, use your nose. Nostril to oil and take a deep breath. Does it smell fresh? Does it evoke the olive grove? Is there a hint of the floral? Is it grassy? Tomatoey? With time you'll learn to differentiate.

If it smells unpleasant, odd, stale or rancid, like a packet of potato chips, don't even consider tasting it. Only proceed to the next stage if you can smell olives in the bouquet.

Fruitiness

If the oil tastes bland, that's not a question mark. That's a failure. Fruitiness means what it says. Can you taste the fruit of the olive? Olives aren't shy. They're strong and bold. This is the easy part.

Bitterness

As with beer, bitterness is a good thing in olive oil, a sign of health-giving properties. Such oil will be good for you. You should taste the bitterness in the front of your mouth.

Those who don't enjoy bitter tastes find olive oil confronting. But if you don't ruin everything with sugar; if you drink lemon, lime and bitters; Campari; bitter ale or green tea, you'll enjoy this characteristic. For many, olive oil is an acquired taste, but well worth the effort.

Be suspicious of brands that claim their olive oil tastes sweet. High-quality extra virgin olive oil is never sweet.

Pungency

This is not so much a taste as a feel. Ever noticed how honey can catch in the back of your throat? Although sweet, honey has pungency. As with honey, this is a sign of quality in olive oil. Pungency is felt *after* the taste. Swish olive oil around in your mouth and you'll notice the pungency a few beats later. It might even make you cough. Pungency is produced by the oil's polyphenols, a group of chemical substances in plants which are believed by some researchers to have beneficial anti-oxidant characteristics. The greater the pungency, the higher the polyphenal percentage, and therefore the greater the nutritional value.

Some aficionados want us to believe that the flavours of olive oil are so precise they should only be married to certain foods. This sort of theatricality might be useful in a restaurant, but at home, good-quality fresh oil can and should be used for just about anything, provided you like the flavour to begin with.

Producers know that the different cultivars have noticeable characteristics: Coratina is usually grassy, Koroneiki is like green bananas, Picual (picked green) is like green tomatoes, Leccino is fruity and Hojiblanco very fruity.

Varieties vary spectacularly in appearance. You only have to look at olives to see why different fruit produces different oils. And if you pick any variety whilst green it will make a different oil than if the fruit is left to ripen to a gleaming black. Even olive pips tell a story; the seeds are just as variable as the fruit.

Colour

The colour of olive oil has surprisingly little bearing on its flavour or quality. In tasting competitions, judges give it no consideration at all. The pigments in the fruit determine the colour. Green olives = green oil. Most olive oils start out green, but as the weeks and months pass they tend to turn yellow. Don't worry. Your oil's not going off - it's simply the chlorophyll converting to other pigments. The higher the polyphenol count, the more likely the oil is to be green, bitter, pungent and robust. Occasionally light yellow oil can be pungent.

Fragrance

Herbaceousness

Spice

Fruitiness

Nuttiness

Greenness

Descriptors

Good olive oil can remind you of . . .

Richard Gawal, presiding judge of the Australian National Olive Oil Show, reminds us that flavour and aroma are not created by the pressing. These are characteristics that come from and are defined by the grove. The simple facts are that the variety of the olive is the principal determinant of the oil, and all olives can produce good oil.

Gawal has created groups to help identify the various flavours in good, complex oil: fragrance, herbaceousness, nuttiness, greenness, spice and fruitiness.

But oil should never remind you of . . .

Now to the vices - the olive oil sins. Let your nose be the guide. Avoid any oil that even hints at blue cheese, vinegar, sour milk, salami, prunes, stale nuts, cucumber or worse - solvent, earth or a 'burnt' flavour.

If any of these flavours are detected in oils submitted for judgement in competitions, the oil is immediately dismissed. The more you learn about olive oil, the more you will realise the importance of trusting your nose and taste.

Tastes to avoid

Setting the standards

To judge the quality of Australian oil we need judges. During the 1990s the industry arranged hundreds of training opportunities for aspiring judges - both professionals and weekend enthusiasts. The Australian Olive Association now has a panel of judges recognised by the IOC (the International Olive Council, based in Madrid), and there are now four shows of national significance and many regional competitions. Beauty quests for extra virgins.

Experienced judges, of which I'm one, volunteer their services. The grandest of the contests is the Australian Olive Association's National Extra Virgin Olive Oil Show. Judged in September, awards are handed out a few weeks later at the industry's annual jamboree, when judges fly into Sydney for two days of tasting and spitting. The boss is the chief steward, responsible for registering all oils, transferring them into opaque bottles and giving them coded labels.

The first test for every entrant is its free fatty acid level. All fats and oils are lipids that are made up of triglyceride molecules - formed by three fatty acids attached to glycerol. When the fatty acids oxidise and break off, becoming 'free', the oil begins deteriorating. The less 'free' fatty acid there is, the better; ie low free fatty acid count equals high oil quality. It must be below .8 per cent to be called extra virgin; fail the test and the oil is disqualified. In 2006 the Australian average was .19 per cent, indicating excellent quality.

Next is the chemical test for polyphenols. Will the oil be placed in the mild, medium or robust category? And variation in the volumes produced by different growers demands a diversity of categories:

Class 1 Single-estate grown; minimum volume 200 litres; mild, medium or robust.
Class 2 Multi-estate grown; 200-4999 litres; mild, medium or robust.
Class 3 Multi-estate grown; greater than 5000 litres; mild, medium or robust.
Class 4 Non-packaged; minimum volume 200 litres.
Class 5 Micro-volume; 50-199 litres.

Class winners are then judged for the 'best in show'.

The industry has a twenty-point scoring system for aroma and taste - fruitiness, bitterness and pungency:

17-20 points	Gold (excellent)
15-16.5 points	Silver (very good)
13-14.5 points	Bronze (above average)

Before tasting, oils are placed in plastic cups. We cover the cup with our hand to slightly warm the oil, lightly swirling it to release the aromas. Then we thrust our noses deep into the cup and breathe in. At home I use wine glasses or tea cups.

Oils are disqualified for smelling fusty, musty, muddy, winey, metallic, rancid or burnt. These negatives are a consequence of contamination during handling. Between tastes we spit out the oil, rinse our mouths with water and if desired, nibble a piece of apple to cleanse our palates. Then we write down the results and reach for the next cup.

Judging notes can read like those of wine tasters. 'Fresh, fruity nose.' 'Complex fresh herbal aromas.' 'Very intense ripe tomato aroma.' 'Good primary fruit characters of bananas.' 'Good late pungency on finish.' 'Moderate confectionery flavours, gingery pungency.' 'Lingering pungency.' 'Honey notes.' 'Spicy flavour matched with a strong, bitter finish.' Scores are added up, consensus reached. Then it's time to award a bronze, a silver, a gold.

Judges are not obliged to give awards at all, but there is usually sufficient enthusiasm for quite a few gongs. Olive oil producer, writer and all-round guru Michael Burr insists that judges should be really fussy. Gold should only be granted when 'fragrance, taste and tactile sensation are in perfect equilibrium.'

It's a good thing to develop olive oil judging skills at home. Organise tasting sessions with your friends; provide spittoons, napkins and palate-cleansing apples. In a world of fast food, it's important to teach your children to focus on the subtleties of taste. I recall a meal in France where the parents questioned their children on ingredients and were proud that they could distinguish the tarragon in the chicken and the nutmeg in the custard. The same skills can be developed to differentiate olive oils.

It is rarely possible to taste an oil before you buy it, although some delicatessans leave samples out in saucers for that purpose. Forget it. After a few hours in the air, they're guaranteed to be awful. And unhygienic. I never dunk those little pieces of stale bread into such oil. Better to pour a few drops fresh from the bottle onto a spoon, sip and swallow.

Chemistry

I now regret dropping out of chemistry before my HSC. These days I'm more interested in the molecular make-up of nutritious foods. There's much discussion about chemistry in human relationships, about the chemistry between actors, but we should be even more concerned with the chemistry of our food.

Fortunately, chemists find extra virgin olive oil particularly intriguing. Attend an international conference on edible oils and the hall will rapidly fill when a scientist discusses the chemical complexities of olive oil. (Other oils seem less compelling. When they're being talked about, scientists take smokos.) Even food chemists who are paid to analyse oils are drawn to the olive beyond simple professional interest, because they enjoy eating it. Perhaps that's why the health benefits of extra virgin olive oil are endlessly discussed in the world's journals.

No matter how much refined oils try to emulate olive oil, the end results are always failures. Stripped to their bare components, refined oils have beta-carotene added and are officially labelled as 'RB&D'. That stands for Refined, Bleached and Deodorised and is as unappetising as it sounds. The edible oil industry demands rigid standardisation. Peanut, safflower, canola, cottonseed and other RB&D oils probably have their place, but they don't have the subtlety, complexity and variety of extra virgin olive oil.

There's a risk that the pressures of international trade and the market push for standardisation will create a 'one size fits all' mentality - a McDonaldisation of extra virgin olive oil's naturalness. Variety must be the spice of our oils.

Australian government laboratories are devoted to understanding the chemical components of olive oils and have long confirmed that Australia's exceed international benchmarks. The oil will undergo an organoleptic test (a scientific assessment of taste). Only if and when the oil meets these chemical and organoleptic benchmarks can it legally be labelled extra virgin.

Oleic acid, a mono-unsaturated fatty acid, is named after the olive. Oils with the highest oleic acid are believed to have the highest nutritional value. This mono-unsaturated fat is particularly stable. There are also saturated and polyunsaturated fats in olive oil. To describe extra virgin olive oil as mono-unsaturated is legal because oleic acid is so dominant. The level of different types of fatty acids in olive oils varies according to where they are grown.

Cooler weather such as Tasmania's produces oil with high levels of mono-unsaturated fats, while Queensland's hotter climate produces olive oil with more saturated fatty acids, such as palmitic and polyunsaturated fats.

However, fatty acid levels are just the beginning of the complexity of extra virgin olive oil. There are the strong anti-oxidants, particularly phenolics, of which there are many different kinds. These decide the bitterness and pungency and whether the oil is considered 'mild', 'medium' or 'robust'. Whilst they are a guide to flavour intensity, these levels are not stand-ardised. Oils with low phenolics can be excellent, but their shelf life is reduced.

Now follows a chorus of other good components, all of which contribute to the mystery of extra virgin olive oil: sterols, hydrocarbons, vitamin E (a-tocopheral), fatty alcohols, chlorophyll, carotenoids, aldehydes, ketones, thiols, alcohols and acids.

In summary, there are more chemical variations between different extra virgin olive oils than between all the other edible oils put together. The important thing to remember is that olive oil is best regarded as a fresh food and should be enjoyed while full of life. That's when you really feel the chemistry.

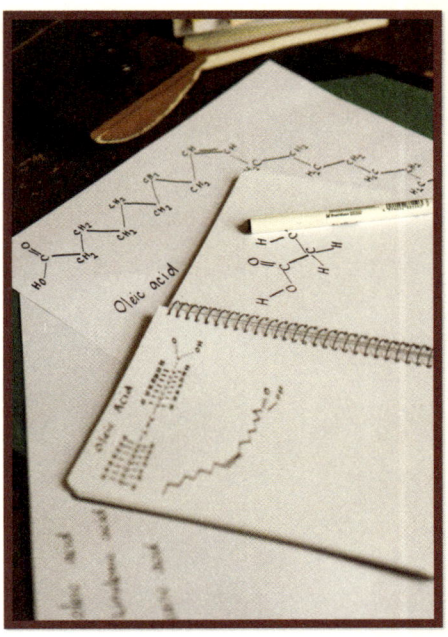

Rancidity

Rancidity is an ugly word much used in the food trade. You can smell it in an old slab of butter or in a fish and chip shop, and you sometimes detect it in nuts left exposed to the elements. Once you've smelt it, the memory lingers like the taste of a bad oyster. Rancidity is a sign of the degradation of food. When it breaks down, a range of volatile components form, giving an undesirable taste and odour.

The main cause of rancidity is old age. In time, all oils will go rancid. How long the process takes depends largely on the polyphenal count when the oil is bottled. A low count means a short life. Rancid olive oil won't kill you, but it tastes dreadful. The best thing to do with rancid olive oil is rub it into your shoes, saddles or other leather goods, wooden tables or tired feet. Forget about eating it.

Olive oil does have an advantage over other oils, however: its high polyphenal count means it goes rancid less quickly than chemically extracted oils, which have no polyphenol count whatsoever. Rancidity will occur more rapidly when oil is exposed to light, heat or air: oil left in clear glass in the hot sun with the lid open can go rancid within hours.

If heat is the enemy of olive oil, does heating oil while cooking reduce the health benefits? No. Olive oil has what's known as a 'high smoke point,'

which refers to the temperature at which an oil creates smoke. Cooking doesn't change good molecules into bad. Hot oil in a pan appears to increase in volume because it's expanding, becoming less viscous and more runny, but on cooling it returns to a thicker state. Just as an egg remains an egg whether it's raw, fried or boiled, your good oil is still good. But don't keep re-using the same oil for frying, as small particles of food left in the oil can burn and emit carcinogens.

Storage

Take a bottle of olive oil in your right hand and say after me: 'Inert glass and stainless steel are best for storing oil.' And store it away from heat and light. Although for this book we've photographed our olive oils in clear glass to emphasise the colours, it's better to use dark bottles in your kitchen. Oxygen kills good oil. That's what oxidisation means: the oil reacts to oxygen and hastens rancidity. In summer I keep my bottles in the fridge. Don't worry if your oil solidifies when you do this; it's simply the saturated fats in the oil hardening. The oil is not harmed in the process - at room temperature the oil will return to its liquid state and the flavour will be unchanged.

How to buy
olive oil

Choice is becoming a chore and profusion generates confusion.
You're standing in your supermarket or health food shop puzzled by dozens
of different brands, all claiming extra virginity. How can you find the perfect
oil? How can you differentiate between good, better or best?

Sadly, labels fudge the truth. Olive oil is as caught up in deceptive packaging as everything else on the market. And not even the most truthful
or beautifully designed label can tell you if you'll like the contents.

The single most important question to ask is: When was the oil pressed?
Forget the 'best before' or recommended 'use-by' date. It's the oil's birthday you
should be checking. If it's not proudly stated on the label, you're in the dark.

The bigger olive groves can take weeks to harvest. The producer may harvest some trees early for a robust oil, then four to six weeks later harvest very
ripe fruit for a milder oil. Every harvest is fraught with difficulties: if it's not
rain, cold snaps or heatwaves, there are problems with getting a team together
or mechanical breakdowns. This means that few oils can correctly claim to
be harvested on such and such a day. Labels that make claims along the lines
of 'harvested in autumn 2007' are probably about as accurate as it gets.

Intelligent consumers need to be sceptical of any claim on any label
in any category. Descriptions tend to be subjective. At best they're guides,

not facts. Since I began working on this book, I've bought scores of Australian olive oils, reading the labels like a biblical scholar studying the Dead Sea scrolls. If you are long-sighted like me, such scholarship isn't always easy. Clearly the reason for making the print on labels so small is to prevent you from reading it. Nonetheless, I have made some discoveries. Some phrases I've found on local labels include 'Australian-owned' and 'Packed in Australia', but do a little detective work and you'll find a cheap imported oil in disguise. If you are seeking Australian olive oil, watch out for phrases like 'Bottled in' or 'Product of'; they don't necessarily tell the truth.

However, the labels must show the official grading, as follows: extra virgin, virgin, pure, pomace and lite.

Extra virgin

An extra virgin label guarantees that the oil came from healthy fruit via clean extraction, that the temperature wasn't too high and the storage hygienic, and that the free fatty acid level was below .8 per cent when bottled. At least you're assured that the oil will be edible. However, official classification focuses on what it must *not* be, not on its quality. Labels set a minimum standard, aiming to banish the defective. The only way you can really tell if you'll like the oil is by tasting it.

Virgin

Oil that tried to be extra virgin but failed. The free fatty acid level is above .8 per cent. It's rarely sold in Australia.

Pure

It's a classic case of the abuse of language. 'Pure' only means that it has not been adulterated with other vegetable oils. The connotations of excellence, wholeness and cleanliness are false. This is factory oil, refined, deodorised and re-blended to bureaucratic standards. It has no place in your kitchen. It is a betrayal of thousands of years of tradition. 'Pure' olive oil is a highly processed oil.

Pomace

Traditionally, the waste product left after the initial pressing for extra virgin olive oil was used for mulch. As olive oil became big business, producers realised there was oil left in the mulch, and one person's waste became another's fortune. They started trucking the waste to factories and mixing it with chemicals to extract every last drop. What results is indeed olive oil, but only just. It is a tasteless fluid which completely lacks the health-giving characteristics of the first pressing. To camouflage this problem, a little dab of extra virgin olive oil is added to give a hint of an aroma. This is the lowest grade and isn't commonly sold in Australia.

Lite

This implies that the product is low-fat. The word is a con - oil is fat. There is no such thing as low-fat oil. Refined and tasteless, 'lite' oil has exactly the same number of kilojoules as any other oil.

Other information

The most exasperating words on any bottle of olive oil are 'Cholesterol-free'. Duh! Cholesterol is only found in animal tissue. All olive oil is entirely free of cholesterol. Hardly a singular achievement.

Other terms used by the industry are often meaningless: premium, superior category, quality A-grade (made from 100 per cent Australian-grown olives) select, first cold press, first pressing, cold-pressed, premium Australian, late harvest, certified authentic, from the finest olives, quality management system certified ISO, best before (often very hard to see), expiry date, unfiltered, bottled in, product of and sweetness. Many of these are nonsense, especially 'late harvest' followed by 'when the oil does not require additional flavour.' Olive oil has flavour. Late harvest is generally milder. But remember, the milder the oil, the shorter the shelf life.

Unfiltered

Unfiltered oil is cloudy because tiny pieces of olive combined with water are left suspended in it. These give the oil extra flavour, but unfiltered oil should be consumed quickly, as these particles speed up the ageing process. Enjoy unfiltered oil as fresh as possible, but be prepared for a thicker, greener oil. The label should show that the oil has been bottled immediately after pressing. Once made, oil is transferred to vats where the olive particles settle. Producers wait a few weeks before opening the valve and pouring the oil straight into bottles. The term for this is 'naturally settled'. Some other oils (but not many) are filtered.

Age

In August 2006, I visited a regional Coles supermarket and bought fifteen of the brands on display. Given the time of year, I could - and should - have been buying some of the 2006 harvest, but not one bottle gave the oil's date of harvest. Some said 'Best before December 2006', whilst others shifted the date to December 2008. I assumed the latter would taste best, but it didn't! Only God and the bottler knew how old those oils were. Although 'robust', 'light', 'fruity' and 'mild' might have been true when the oil was bottled, these desirable characteristics may be long gone when you unscrew the cap. Especially when the oil's birthday is a closely guarded secret.

Nutritional information

It is compulsory to list nutritional information on all packaged food. The categories that must be covered are:

- Protein
- Fat: Total
  - Saturated
  - Poly
  - Mono
- Cholesterol
- Carbohydrate
- Sugars
- Sodium
- Potassium

But olive oil only has fat in it - saturated, poly and mono, to give you a total fat count. There's no protein, carbohydrate, sugar or salt in it.

How is olive oil made?

Before food became as mass-produced as cars, making olive oil couldn't have been simpler. The fruit was crushed beneath massive stone wheels, the paste spread between straw mats for pressing. The oil would dribble down into a container and be transferred into pots.

Pick ripe, healthy fruit. Crush it straight away. Behold, the premium product: extra virgin olive oil. Should you choose poor-quality fruit, let it bake in the sun, go a little mouldy in the pickers' baskets, or process it insensitively, oil loses its virginity.

Today, Australian olives are put into stainless steel continuous processing machines. Olives in. Oil out. Olives are delivered, washed, crushed with a hammer mill and turned in a malaxer where the paste is churned for about an hour before entering a separator. Water and olive solids go one way, while olive oil pours into the stainless steel vat. The process is still simple.

Regions

Australian olive oil is made in almost every agricultural region except the tropics - and every region claims that theirs is the best. Australia's olive oil harvest can start in Queensland in February and end as late as August in the cooler regions of Victoria and Tasmania. Fresh oils from the warmer regions can be on the market the day after they are made, but oils pressed in the cooler regions take time to settle and can often take longer to reach market.

What about blending?

As in the wine industry, olive oil producers try to extend supplies, create styles and maintain consistency and, inevitably, some of them blend different varieties of olives to achieve this. Blended extra virgin olive oil contains no other vegetable oils. Blending simply refers to joining together top-quality extra virgin oils.

As Richard Gawal says, 'a good oil can be lost in a bad blend', yet many award-winning oils *are* blended. For less noble reasons (that is, to drive down costs), most supermarket oils are blends.

However, many of us are proud to produce a singular oil from a single grove. This guarantees individuality and diversity.

Other uses

My favourite scene in *The Life of Brian* is when a radical critic of Rome asks the famous rhetorical question 'What have the Romans done for us?' The answers included 'roads' and 'aqueducts'. Paraphrasing that, let's ask what olive oil can do for us. The answers include food, fuel, lighting, lubricants, moisturiser and medicines; the list will lengthen during the twenty-first century.

It's already being used to lubricate snowboards and cricket bats. Our leather saddles, boots, belts and wooden tables all get a regular rub-down - a small dab of oil on a damp cloth is sufficient. Fastidious cleaners put a teaspoon with a squeeze of lemon in the bucket to wash parquetry floors.

Phillip has been known to use it to grease a squeaky door, and I dab it on my secateurs blade. A friend rubs it into her hair before entering a sauna and I always put a few drops into my ear if I get an earache.

It's an effective exfoliant if you use it with salt to rub over your feet. We only ever use 100 per cent homemade olive oil soap on our skin, and when I bring home the first pressing of the season, I stuff my pillow into an old slip and massage olive oil all over my face and neck for a totally luxurious sleep.

The future

At last count, Australia had nine million olive trees in the ground. Many of these are still youngsters, but they should be in full production by 2010. Currently, productivity has been damaged by frost and drought and we have a few problems unknown to the Romans and our international competitors - the likes of kangaroos, cockatoos and currawongs.

Nine million sounds like a lot of trees, but it represents a miniscule .7 per cent of the world's olive industry. Our groves range from small producers with a few hundred trees to corporate giants with 500,000. Even a grove of that size is small by world standards. If we achieve 1 per cent of world production over the next twenty years, we'll barely rate as a boutique industry. Yet a long history of Australian success in horticulture suggests we could become a force to be reckoned with, provided we focus on quality. There's always been a shortage of good olive oil (most olive oil traded is 'pure'), and Australia can help fill the gap.

We'll find an important role in international markets - as a minor player, perhaps, but a reliable source. For example, Australian producers are very pernickety about damaged fruit. In contrast to Europe, where everything goes into the mincer, we're choosy about the fruit that makes the grade. That's one reason why around 97 per cent of Australian oil is pretty damn good.

The concept of traceability from farm to kitchen is becoming ever more important in all forms of food production. If there's ever a problem in this modern version of the food chain, we need to be able to backtrack, to rewind, to find out what went wrong and where. Traceability with olive oil is one of the benefits of a young industry. We've incorporated good systems from the beginning, whereas despite increasing EU regulations, the older industries are yet to offer such guarantees.

Future growth will be affected by our dramas with water. Most Australian groves are irrigated and watering has created our trademark 'fruitiness'. Watering reduces bitterness, so if our olives have to survive with less water we'll be tasting more bitter oils.

Australia produces some of the fruitiest olive oils in the world, and international tasters often talk of a 'pleasant experience'. We can't quantify that chemically, but it's part of the taste process and it's good the world likes it. Our growing sales in Spain and Italy are a significant achievement, and it's a pleasure seeing Australian oil on the shelves in Rome.

Genetically modified food

I turn to Shakespeare for the words to express my admonishment against genetically modified food. It's there, loud and clear: 'By the pricking of my thumbs, something wicked this way comes.' Memorable words from *Macbeth*. The witches are gathered around their cauldron, urgently trying to improve on 6 billion years of evolution by mixing together a macabre variety of ingredients: 'Eye of newt and toe of frog, wool of bat and tongue of dog.' On and on the recipe goes, adding adders, worms, lizards and various pieces of human being.

Whilst there are strong arguments for genetic modification in medicine, where the experiments are largely quarantined within the human body, I've always opposed letting it loose in agriculture. Quarantining has proved impossible, traditional farming is being destroyed.

Genetic modification is already well established in oil-producing crops like canola, soy, corn and cotton (cottonseed oil is used to fry Australian potato chips) - and no farm, no matter how organic, can be safe from genetically modified pollen and seed drift polluting its paddocks. Having already damaged food quality with chemicals, pesticides and hormones, industrial agriculturalists and processed food corporations can't wait to transform everything we eat by cutting and pasting the genetic codes of flora and fauna,

mixing plant, animal and insect in combinations that would have *Macbeth*'s witches dancing with delight and cackling approval.

Many, many thousands of years of evolution have gone into olives, with farmers playing chess with varieties, soils and seasons. Genetic modi-fication is determined to cheat at this game, effecting more change in a decade than in all of history. The risks are enormous. That's why I hope that the olive tree can fight off the challenge - that those who love the oil will protect the fruit from this Frankensteinian fiddling. We don't mind the toil, but keep the double trouble out of our groves and bottles. Olive oil today is 100 per cent free from genetic modification.

Come into my kitchen

When I bring home the first batch of new season oil, fresh and unfiltered, I fill the small jug we usually use for milk and pass it around as reverently as if it were the chalice at the Last Supper. This thick green fluid feels every bit as precious as sacred wine.

Is there anything olive oil doesn't go with? Well, I wouldn't pour it on fruit salad, but it's delicious on salads of oranges and onions. It's probably too strong for a crème brûlée, but it's perfect for baking Christmas cake. My salads, vegetables, dips and tidbits

continue to evolve as I learn to be generous and take risks. It's magical what just a few drops can do.

Be abundant with oil - not to add more kilojoules but to enhance the flavour of every ingredient. Phillip has a memory from his days in advertising, when a man from Heinz admitted to him that tomato sauce wasn't about taste; rather, 'people use it as a moisturiser.' Evidently we prefer wet food to dry food. So let olive oil be the new tomato sauce, albeit with real taste.

Breads and savoury baked goods

Poor old bread. It's come under sustained attack by the no-carb brigade - first cousins of the low-fat loonies. Slices, rolls and focaccias have been driven from the dining table. As a woman of a certain age, I do find myself cutting back, but I will never abandon bread, the most fundamental and wonderful of foods.

I can't resist fresh bread with fresh olive oil. They go together like young lovers or old friends. No two people eat bread and butter the same way - they like different thicknesses of bread, or tear a roll open with a flourish; some put butter on in thick slabs, others spread it smoothly. So it is with bread and olive oil. Give your family and friends a choice. Let them choose from fresh or toasted bread. Let them rub it with garlic or sprinkle it with rock salt. Let them pour the oil directly onto the bread or dip the bread into a dish of oil.

Electric breadmakers have made baking easy and I've yet to meet a kid who doesn't love using them. Plonk flour, salt, olive oil and yeast into the machine and let it make a dough. Lay it on your bench, flatten it out focaccia-style, let it rise, and bake it in the oven. Or cook the whole thing in the machine.

When I don't bake my own bread I insist on the best available. Until recently, our local shops only stocked bread that tastes like sliced Wettex. Then the gods smiled on us - a brilliant baker arrived from Puglia to live and work in the region. While some purists think sourdough is too strong to be served with fresh olive oil, everyone agrees you need real bread, not mushy sandwich loaves softened with soy flour. If your bread stays 'fresh' in the kitchen for days, ditch it.

If your neighbourhood doesn't boast a friendly baker from Puglia, try some of the simple bread recipes on the following pages.

Baguettes with anchovies

While visiting an olive grove in Sicily we were served baguettes to remember. They'd been cut in half, drenched in fresh oil, filled with anchovies, closed up, sliced into chunks and wrapped in white paper napkins. We'd been sampling oil in cups and it had been so pungent that our noses wrinkled involuntarily. Now that same oil, soaked into the baguette, was aromatic and romantic. Served with a simple salad, this combination lets you recreate that feeling in your own kitchen.

Cut baguette in half lengthwise. Pour olive oil generously over the inside, then fill with anchovies. Close up baguette, cut into 6 cm pieces and serve wrapped in white paper napkins with a green salad to the side.

1 baguette

olive oil for drizzling

100 g jar anchovies, drained

SERVES 4

Tomato and basil bruschetta

This recipe may be the most widely known rendition of bruschetta, but at its simplest, bruschetta is just slices of good wood-fired bread toasted or grilled over open flames, rubbed with a cut clove of garlic and drizzled with your best extra virgin olive oil.

6 large vine-ripened tomatoes, seeded and roughly chopped

2 cloves garlic, 1 halved and 1 finely chopped

sea salt and freshly ground black pepper

12 × 2 cm thick slices sourdough

extra virgin olive oil for brushing

¹/₃ cup torn basil

aged balsamic vinegar (optional) for drizzling

Place tomatoes and chopped garlic in a bowl, season with salt and pepper and leave for 10 minutes. Grill bread on a hot grill plate or barbecue until toasted. Rub each slice with a halved garlic clove, then liberally brush with olive oil. Top bread slices with tomato mixture and scatter over basil. Drizzle over a little more olive oil and balsamic vinegar if desired.

SERVES 6

66

Stephanie Alexander's
Pizza bianca with herbs

To make garnish, place garlic and herbs in a bowl and cover with olive oil. Set aside to infuse.

To make dough, dissolve yeast in water, leave for 10 minutes and then mix with flour, sea salt and olive oil. Turn out dough onto a lightly floured surface and knead vigorously for 10 minutes. The dough should be very light and slightly sticky. Place in a lightly oiled bowl, cover with a damp tea towel and leave in a draught-free place to rise for 1 hour.

Preheat oven to 220°C.

Divide dough into three even pieces and rest on a lightly floured surface for 15 minutes. Pat and stretch each piece into a long slipper shape and place on an oiled baking tray. The surface should be dimpled from the action of your fingers on the soft dough. Brush generously with most of the garnish and put into the oven immediately. Bake until golden - about 10-15 minutes. Remove from oven and brush with the rest of the garnish. Scatter with a little sea salt if desired.

Pizza bianca is best served immediately, but can be reheated quickly on a hotplate or in a heavy frying pan. There is no need to add any oil to the pan.

MAKES 3 PIZZAS

Garnish
2 cloves garlic, **roughly chopped**
2 tablespoons roughly chopped rosemary *or* basil
½ cup extra virgin olive oil, plus extra for oiling bowl and tray

Pizza dough
10 g fresh yeast *or* 5 g dry yeast
300 ml lukewarm water
500 g strong plain flour
2 teaspoons sea salt, plus extra to serve
1 tablespoon extra virgin olive oil

This recipe was described to Stephanie by chef Kingsley Sullivan as he demonstrated bread-making at the century-old bakery of the monastery at New Norcia in Western Australia.

Olive and rosemary bread

This bread can be eaten on its own; it doesn't require any embellishments, other than a bowl of peppery extra virgin olive oil for dipping. It keeps well for a few days and is delicious toasted and topped with fetta and sliced tomatoes.

Combine flour, yeast and salt in a large bowl, then add egg and water and, using clean hands, mix to form a firm dough. Turn out dough onto a floured surface and knead for 5 minutes. Coat the inside of a large, clean bowl with a little olive oil, then place dough in the bowl and pour over 1 tablespoon olive oil. Cover loosely with plastic film and leave in a draught-free place for 2 hours or until dough has doubled in size.

Transfer dough to a floured bench and knock it back, then knead for 5 minutes. Spread it out and sprinkle over olives, rosemary and 2 teaspoons olive oil, then knead them in for another 5 minutes. Transfer dough to a clean, oiled bowl and pour on another tablespoon of oil. Cover loosely with plastic film and leave in a draught-free place to rise again for another hour.

Preheat oven to 200°C and place two heavy baking trays inside it while it heats. Place dough on a floured bench and divide in half, then shape into two long loaves. Place each loaf on a piece of baking paper (this will help you transfer them to the baking trays) and lightly brush with the egg wash. Bake for 35 minutes or until the loaves sound hollow when tapped with your fingers.

Olive and rosemary bread keeps well for up to 3 days. It can be frozen for up to 1 month.

MAKES 2 LOAVES

1 kg strong plain flour

2 tablespoons dry yeast

1 tablespoon sea salt

4 eggs, beaten

2 cups lukewarm water

¼ cup extra virgin olive oil

250 g Kalamata olives, pitted
   and roughly chopped

2 tablespoons chopped
   rosemary

1 egg, beaten with
   1 tablespoon milk

Russell Jeavons'
Dukkah with handmade bread and olive oil

Preheat oven to 150°C. Toast almonds for about 10 minutes, taking care not to burn them. Test them by breaking an almond in half; they are ready when golden inside. Set aside to cool.

Toast sesame, coriander and fennel seeds separately for a few minutes on baking trays in the oven until lightly toasted and aromatic - again, be careful not to burn them. Set aside to cool.

When almonds are cool, grind them carefully in a food processor. The texture should vary from pieces the size of a match head down to fine crumbs. Be very careful not to over-grind or you will end up with almond paste.

When seeds are cool, grind them separately. The sesame seeds only need to be broken, rather than ground finely, and this can be done using a mortar and pestle or in a food processor. The coriander and fennel seeds need to be ground into a fine powder, which can be done using a mortar and pestle or a coffee grinder.

Mix all the ground ingredients together with the salt and pepper.

Serve the oil and dukkah in separate bowls with the bread; the bread is dipped in the oil and then in the dukkah. Store any leftovers in an airtight container. The dukkah will keep in good condition for up to 3 months.

MAKES 2-3 CUPS

500 g almonds, skins on
125 g sesame seeds
60 g coriander seeds
1 tablespoon wild
   fennel seeds
1/4 teaspoon salt
1/4 teaspoon freshly ground
   black pepper
extra virgin olive oil
   to serve
1 loaf handmade bread,
   such as sourdough or
   ciabatta, cut into bite-
   sized pieces

Traditionally, dukkah is served on a plate, with a pot of extra virgin olive oil and bite-sized pieces of handmade bread on the side. It is also delicious with fresh goat's curd and vegetable crudités.

Russell Jeavons'
House favourite pizza

Pizza dough

500 g unbleached
bread flour

150 g stone-ground
wholemeal flour

1/2 teaspoon dry yeast

1 teaspoon sea salt

approximately 400 ml
filtered water, half
boiling, half cold

Topping

1/2 cup tomato passata
or 2 tomatoes, diced

1 cup pitted black olives

1 clove garlic

few drops balsamic vinegar

extra virgin olive oil for
brushing and drizzling

1 cup diced tomatoes or
halved cherry tomatoes

handful of fresh basil
leaves, plus extra
to serve

4 tablespoons grated
parmesan

400 g buffalo mozzarella,
cut into 1 cm slices

To make dough, mix flours and yeast on a flat surface and form a well in the centre. Dissolve salt in 200 ml boiling filtered water, then add remaining cold water. Allow it to cool to body temperature (although if the ingredients are cold or it is a very cold day, the water needs to be hotter, as we are working towards body-temperature dough). Pour it into the well, using one hand to gather in the flour, making a paste at first and then a dough. Keep one hand free for adding more water or flour. When dough is cohesive but wet and sticky, begin to knead with both hands. Keep a plastic pastry scraper handy to scrape dough from the bench and your hands. Continue folding and turning until a smooth, cohesive, easy-to-work dough has formed.

Place dough in a steep-sided container like a bucket or saucepan. If the kitchen is cold, put the dough somewhere warm. If it is very cold, put it in a sink of warm water. Prove for 1-2 hours. Divide dough into quarters and form into 4 balls. Rest for 10 minutes.

If you are using diced tomatoes instead of passata, cook them in a saucepan over a medium heat for half an hour, crushing tomatoes as they cook, then strain off excess liquid. Preheat oven to 240°C.

To make olive paste, blend olives with garlic and balsamic vinegar using a mortar and pestle or a food processor.

Roll or press out each dough ball into a 25 cm disc and brush with olive oil. Spread tomato sauce or passata, not too evenly, over dough, then sprinkle on tomatoes, basil and parmesan. Place mozzarella in rounds on top. Put some blobs of olive paste in several places.

Cook pizzas for 10-12 minutes. Serve scattered with basil leaves and a generous drizzle of olive oil.

MAKES 4 PIZZAS

Inspired by the great pizzas of Napoli, Russell has added olive paste to complement the olive oil. As with all pizza, keep it simple and uncrowded and cook it hot. If you have a wood-fired oven, cook it directly on the bricks.

Pastry

200 g plain flour
70 ml extra virgin olive oil
50 g grated parmesan
1 teaspoon sea salt
2-3 tablespoons water

Filling

3 red onions, finely sliced
150 ml extra virgin olive oil
1 teaspoon honey
2 tablespoons balsamic
    vinegar
sea salt and freshly ground
    black pepper to taste
1 red capsicum (pepper),
    sliced into 2.5 cm strips
1 yellow capsicum (pepper),
    sliced into 2.5 cm strips
2 cloves garlic, finely sliced
20 Kalamata olives, pitted
handful of basil, chopped

Rachel Grisewood's
Yellow and red capsicum tarts with olive oil pastry

Add all pastry ingredients, except water, to a food processor and process until the mixture is the consistency of rough breadcrumbs. Add water, continuing to process until dough just comes together. Turn out dough onto a lightly floured surface. Cover with plastic film and cool in the refrigerator for 30 minutes.

To prepare filling, place onion in a saucepan with 75 ml of the olive oil and cook, covered, over a low heat for about 1 hour. Add honey and vinegar and cook until thick and unctuous. Season with salt and pepper. Add red and yellow capsicum and garlic with remaining oil and cook over a low heat with lid on until capsicum is soft. Season with salt and pepper.

Preheat oven to 180°C and grease and line a baking tray with baking paper. Roll out pastry on a lightly floured surface until it is 5 mm thick. With a 5 cm round cutter, cut 20 circles from the pastry, lift them onto baking tray and, using a fork, prick each circle a couple of times. Bake in the oven for 5 minutes until the edges are just turning golden.

Spoon onion and capsicum mixture over each tart and top with an olive. Bake for another 20 minutes. Remove tarts from oven, sprinkle with some basil and serve with a green salad as an entrée or as a main course with a tomato and buffalo mozzarella salad, such as the Caprese Salad on page 145.

MAKES 20 TARTS

The pastry here is very crisp, perfect for the rich filling. The leftovers are wonderful cold – just the thing for a picnic.

Dips and sauces

Dips make a great snack with bread or crackers, or they can be served as side dishes with main meals. Pesto goes well with sausages and mash, as do white bean dip, and capsicum and fetta dip. For dipping, I tear pita bread into odd shapes, lay the pieces on a tray and dry-bake them in a hot oven for 5 minutes. Crisped up, they're ready to dip.

If you're in a hurry, a salsa (Spanish and Italian for 'sauce') can be a good alternative to a more complicated sauce. The reputation of salsas has suffered because of the supermarket product sold with tacos, but they can be wonderful. I make loads of variations to complement meat.

Jo Jo's dip

This dip is great made with fresh peas, but it's equally delicious if you use dried green split peas.

1 cup podded peas *or* ³/₄ cup dried split green peas

5 large spinach leaves

3 large cloves garlic, crushed

juice of 2 large lemons

¹/₃ cup chopped flat-leaf parsley

140 g tahini

sea salt and freshly ground black pepper

extra virgin olive oil for drizzling

If using dried green split peas, wash well in water and soak overnight before cooking. Cook peas in a saucepan of boiling water until tender (about 5 minutes if fresh or 30-40 minutes if dried), skimming off any scum that floats to the surface, then drain and leave to cool. Lightly blanch spinach in a saucepan of boiling water, then drain and squeeze out excess moisture.

Process all ingredients except olive oil in a blender or food processor until a smooth purée forms. Transfer to a bowl and chill.

Serve dip with extra virgin olive oil drizzled over it.

MAKES ABOUT 1 ³/₄ CUPS

White bean dip

This is one of my favourite dips. Serve it with crusty sourdough bread or barbecued lamb.

Process all ingredients in a food processor or blender until a smooth purée forms. Adjust seasoning, transfer to a bowl, drizzle generously with extra virgin olive oil and serve.

MAKES ABOUT 1 CUP

1 × 400 g tin cannellini beans, drained
1 clove garlic, crushed
1/2 cup chopped basil, mint *or* flat-leaf parsley
juice of 1 lemon
1 teaspoon ground cumin
2 tablespoons water
sea salt and freshly ground black pepper
2 tablespoons extra virgin olive oil, plus extra for drizzling

Capsicum and fetta dip

The strong, salty flavour of fetta pairs beautifully with the robust sweetness of roasted red capsicums. Simplicity at its best.

Cut capsicums into quarters and remove seeds. Arrange capsicum on a baking tray, skin-side up, and cook under a hot grill until skins blacken and blister. Place in a plastic bag and leave for 5 minutes - the steam helps loosen the skins, making them easier to peel. Peel capsicums and slice thinly.

Process capsicum, garlic and fetta in a food processor until a purée forms. Transfer to a bowl, then drizzle with extra virgin olive oil and serve.

MAKES ABOUT 1 3/4 CUPS

3 red capsicums (peppers)
1 clove garlic, crushed
125 g fetta, diced
extra virgin olive oil for drizzling

Greg Malouf's
Split pea dip with olives and goat's cheese

1 onion, finely diced

1/3 cup extra virgin olive oil

2 cloves garlic, finely
   chopped

200 g green split peas,
   soaked overnight in
   cold water

1/3 whole nutmeg, grated

sea salt and freshly ground
   black pepper

80 g goat's cheese, roughly
   crumbled

10 large black olives, pitted
   and roughly chopped

In a large saucepan, sauté onion in half of the olive oil over a low heat until it is soft and transparent, taking care not to let it colour. Add garlic and sauté for a few more minutes.

Pour in split peas and enough water to cover the peas by two finger-widths. Bring to the boil, then reduce heat to low and allow to simmer gently for 30-40 minutes, until peas have broken down to a green mush and the water has nearly evaporated. Season mixture with nutmeg, salt and pepper, and allow it to cool slightly.

Whisk remaining olive oil into the mix, and fold through goat's cheese and olives. Adjust the seasoning and allow to cool completely. Serve with plenty of fresh Lebanese flat bread.

MAKES ABOUT 1 1/2 CUPS

Adding the strong flavours of black olives and goat's cheese makes this a knock-out. And it's all brought together by the final addition of olive oil.

Salsa verde

I rarely hear about salsa verde any more but I like its pure and humble flavour. Traditionally used to enliven simple dishes, it is ideal served with barbecued or roasted beef, lamb or fish, or tossed through warm chargrilled summer vegetables such as eggplant, zucchini and capsicum and topped with crumbled goat's cheese.

2 anchovy fillets, chopped

1 tablespoon salted capers, rinsed and drained

2 large cloves garlic, finely chopped

1/2 cup firmly packed flat-leaf parsley, chopped

1/4 cup firmly packed mint, chopped

1/4 cup firmly packed basil, chopped

2 teaspoons red-wine vinegar

2 teaspoons Dijon mustard

1/3 cup extra virgin olive oil

sea salt and freshly ground black pepper

Process all ingredients except olive oil, salt and pepper in a food processor until well combined, then, with the motor running, add the olive oil in a thin, steady stream and process until smooth. Season with salt and freshly ground black pepper.

Salsa verde will keep for up to 3 days in the refrigerator, closely covered with plastic film or in an airtight container.

MAKES 3/4 CUP

Baba ghanoush

The olio nuovo (new oil) season coincides with the full ripening of eggplant. This classic Middle Eastern dip is a perfect way to show off the unique qualities of eggplant — its smoky flavour and silky texture.

Cook eggplant whole in a covered barbecue over a medium heat for 10 minutes, then turn and cook for another 10 minutes or until tender. Alternatively, you can roast it at 200°C for 30 minutes. Drain in a colander for 30 minutes; eggplant flesh emits a lot of liquid when cooked, so this needs to be drained off. The eggplant will collapse as it cooks and drains.

Peel eggplant, discard any large seeds and chop roughly. Process eggplant in a food processor with garlic, cumin, tahini, lemon juice and olive oil until a smooth paste forms. Season with salt and pepper.

Transfer to a bowl, sprinkle with sumac and drizzle with a little more olive oil. Serve with fresh Lebanese flat bread.

MAKES ABOUT 2 CUPS

2 large eggplants (aubergines), pricked with a fork
2 large cloves garlic, finely chopped
1/2 teaspoon ground cumin
2 1/2 tablespoons tahini
juice of 1 lemon
1/4 cup extra virgin olive oil, plus extra to serve
sea salt and freshly ground black pepper
sumac to serve

Rouille

This classic French sauce is traditionally served with bouillabaisse (see page 114).

Roast, peel and seed capsicum (see recipe on page 79 for detailed instructions). Place all ingredients except oil in a food processor and purée. Add the oil in a thin stream with the motor running and when the mixture thickens, pass through a fine sieve.

MAKES ABOUT 2 CUPS

1 red capsicum (pepper)
1 medium potato, boiled and peeled
4 cloves garlic, crushed
1/2 teaspoon cayenne pepper
3 egg yolks
50 ml white vinegar
sea salt and freshly ground black pepper
200 ml extra virgin olive oil

Pesto

40 g pine nuts
2 cloves garlic
sea salt
1 ½ cups firmly packed
    torn basil
⅔ cup extra virgin olive oil
40 g grated parmesan
20 g grated pecorino
freshly ground black pepper

Pesto was originally made in Genoa using fresh basil, pine nuts, garlic, olive oil and parmesan cheese, but all kinds of variations are possible, using coriander, rocket or mint, for example. You can use different kinds of nuts – I prefer Australian macadamia nuts; the important thing is always to use good-quality olive oil. Pesto is delicious tossed through pasta, spread on bread or used to garnish soup.

Preheat oven to 150°C. Roast pine nuts on a baking tray for 6-8 minutes or until fragrant. Leave to cool.

Using the flat of a large knife, crush garlic and ½ teaspoon salt on a chopping board to form a paste, then transfer to a food processor. Add basil and pine nuts and process until finely chopped, then, with the motor running, add olive oil in a thin, steady stream and process until a smooth paste forms. Stir in cheeses and season to taste.

Pesto will keep for up to 3 days in the refrigerator, in an airtight container or a bowl closely covered with plastic film. It can be stored in the freezer for up to 1 month - omit the cheese, then stir it through the defrosted pesto just before using.

MAKES ABOUT 1 CUP

Belinda Jeffery's
Tomato and olive salsa

Seed and dice tomatoes. Pit and slice olives. Stir all ingredients except salt together in a bowl, then season with salt to taste and set aside for about half an hour to allow the flavours to develop fully.

MAKES ABOUT 3 CUPS

4 ripe tomatoes
120 g Kalamata olives
1 red onion, finely chopped
1 clove garlic, finely chopped
$\frac{1}{4}$ cup extra virgin olive oil
2 teaspoons balsamic vinegar
2-3 teaspoons thyme or
    1 tablespoon torn basil
sea salt

This salsa was created to go with the crunchy parmesan chicken on page 190, but it is also delicious served as a dip with crackers.

Bagna cauda

This Piedmontese specialty is a great way to use your best extra virgin olive oil. It is literally a hot, garlicky, anchovy-spiked bath for dipping raw, blanched or roasted vegetables.

Process olive oil, butter, anchovies and garlic in a food processor until smooth. Heat mixture in a small saucepan over a very low heat (use a simmer mat, if necessary) for 10 minutes, stirring frequently, taking care not to let it boil. Season with pepper and serve immediately (otherwise the bagna cauda may separate) with vegetables of your choice for dipping.

MAKES ABOUT 1½ CUPS

$^3/_4$ cup extra virgin olive oil
120 g unsalted butter, chopped
8 anchovy fillets, chopped
5-6 large cloves garlic, chopped
freshly ground black pepper

Infusions, vinaigrettes and marinades

Infusions

Although I used to disapprove of purchased infusions (it's so easy to make them at home), it has to be admitted that some are very good - those that blend high-quality extracts of herbs or spices into fine extra virgin olive oil before bottling. There are now many kinds of infused oils on the market, from the more common garlic, basil and chilli to those with native Australian additions such as pepper-berry and lemon myrtle. Unfortunately these flavourings are often added during pressing, which affects the oil's shelf life. The flavour is powerful and delicious but they need to be consumed promptly. Read all labels carefully when buying.

I sometimes keep a few small jars of good oil with herbs stuffed into them: rosemary to brush over potato, basil to pour over tomato, garlic for everything, chilli for chicken, and tarragon for eggs. If I'm really honest I mainly do it because I like the look of fresh herbs in olive oil. I rarely use infusions unless making a special meal, but infusing the oil does give a more refined appearance and a subtler flavour than simply drizzling oil with chunks of herbs in it over food. However, if you want a quick result, just brush whatever you're cooking with olive oil and add chopped herbs.

You can make infused oil at home and there's no doubt that the final result is a sophisticated product. Greg Malouf uses infused oil with preserved lemons to great effect, and the basil-infused olive oil recipe I give on page 92 is delicious with pasta and all kinds of vegetables. I highly recommend you try infusing olive oil at least once to see what can be achieved. Just remember *never* to use old olive oil. Even herbs won't disguise rancidity.

Vinaigrettes

Freshly gathered salad greens often appear on my table over the warmer months, and it is easy to make them more than just an adjunct to the meal with a home-made vinaigrette. You just need a supply of good olive oil and quality vinegar in your pantry.

The general rule is to use one part acidulant (either one of the many types of vinegar available, such as balsamic, red or white wine, or sherry; or citrus juice, such as lemon, lime or tangerine) to three to four parts oil. One of the simplest and best dressings possible is a tablespoon of balsamic vinegar drizzled over salad greens, followed by a quarter of a cup of olive oil. Toss to combine.

Use just enough dressing to coat the leaves - there shouldn't be a pool of dressing at the base of the bowl or the salad will become soggy. The recipes here will be enough to dress 200 g salad leaves, which should serve 4. Try rocket, lettuce, watercress, baby spinach leaves or endive, or a mixture of these, and make sure the leaves are washed and well dried, using a salad spinner if you have one, or wrapping them in a tea towel if you don't. If the leaves are wet, the dressing won't cling to them properly. Always add the dressing just before serving.

Marinades

Marinades add an extra dimension of flavour to meat, poultry and seafood by infusing them with the essence of the marinade ingredients. They also tenderise meat and keep it moist during the cooking process. This is important when you're using a dry heat source such as the barbecue.

There's great scope for creativity. As long as you have excellent extra virgin olive oil and some herbs and garlic, you have the basics of a great marinade. If you add honey or sugar, it is best to barbecue or grill over a lower heat and for a little longer than usual, to ensure that the meat cooks through without the exterior burning.

Marinate beef, lamb and pork overnight if you have time, and for 2 hours at least. A minimum of 30 minutes and a maximum of a couple of hours is fine for imparting flavours to poultry, which does not need to be tenderised. Fish and prawns only need to be marinated for 10-20 minutes, due to the less sinuous structure of the flesh and a lack of connective tissue and muscle; don't marinate them for any longer, as the marinade will start to 'cook' the flesh. However, octopus and squid can withstand a longer marinating time (anywhere from 2 hours to overnight), particularly if wine or an acidic ingredient is used, as they will help tenderise it.

If you plan to serve the leftover marinade as a sauce, it needs to be cooked first to prevent food poisoning.

Basil-infused olive oil

*This oil is delicious added to vinaigrettes,
or drizzled over tomato soup, roasted capsicums,
pasta, fish or seafood. To make other herb-infused
oils, use the same quantity of soft herbs such as
tarragon, flat-leaf parsley or coriander. For woody
herbs, such as rosemary or sage, use 1 cup packed
leaves to 2 cups extra virgin olive oil.*

3 cups firmly packed basil
1 ½ cups extra virgin olive oil

Plunge basil into a saucepan of boiling water for 5 seconds, then drain well, squeeze out all the moisture and pat dry with paper towel. Process basil and olive oil in a food processor until a purée forms. Strain oil through a fine sieve, then through a muslin-lined sieve; do not press down on the solids as this will cloud the oil.

Transfer to a sterilised 500 ml bottle and seal. Basil oil is best stored in the refrigerator and used within 1 week.

NOTE: To sterilise containers, wash them in hot, soapy water, then place them on a baking tray in a 120°C oven for 25-30 minutes. This will prevent harmful bacteria from developing.

MAKES ABOUT 2 CUPS

Greg Malouf's
Preserved lemon olive oil

Scrape flesh from preserved lemons and discard. Finely dice skins and place in a sterilised 500 ml jar with fresh lemon quarters, coriander seeds and black peppercorns.

In a saucepan, gently warm olive oil over a low heat to blood temperature (just warm) and pour over lemons. Seal jar tightly and allow to sit, undisturbed, for 3 days.

Strain oil through a clean tea towel placed over a bowl. Allow it to drain naturally - don't be tempted to push it through, as this will cloud the oil. Pour into a sterilised bottle, reseal and use as desired. This infused oil will keep for up to 1 week in a cool, dark cupboard.

NOTE: To sterilise containers, wash them in hot, soapy water, then place them on a baking tray in a 120°C oven for 25-30 minutes. This will prevent harmful bacteria from developing.

MAKES ABOUT 1 $\frac{1}{4}$ CUPS

2 preserved lemons
2 lemons, cut into quarters
1 teaspoon crushed coriander seeds
$\frac{1}{2}$ teaspoon crushed black peppercorns
1 cup extra virgin olive oil

Preserved lemon olive oil makes a surprisingly tangy change in vinaigrettes and salad dressings, or drizzle it straight onto fish or poultry after grilling.

Traditional vinaigrette

1 tablespoon Dijon mustard

2 1/2 tablespoons aged red-wine
    vinegar

2 small cloves garlic, finely
    chopped

sea salt and freshly ground
    black pepper

1/2 cup extra virgin olive oil

1 tablespoon chopped flat-leaf
    parsley

Combine mustard, vinegar and garlic in a bowl, season with salt and
pepper, then slowly whisk in olive oil until well combined. Add parsley
and stir through.

MAKES ABOUT 3/4 CUP

Lemon and marjoram vinaigrette

juice of 1 lemon

1/3 cup extra virgin olive oil

1 lemon, flesh seeded and
    pulped, rind finely grated

2 tablespoons chopped
    marjoram

sea salt and freshly ground
    black pepper

Whisk together lemon juice and olive oil. Stir in lemon pulp,
lemon rind and marjoram, then season with salt and pepper.

MAKES ABOUT 1/2 CUP

Marinated olives with rosemary, orange and fennel seed

Make sure the oil you use to marinate your olives is as fresh as you'd use for any other purpose. Sometimes people use stale, rancid olive oil for marinating olives and totally ruin them.

Lightly crush coriander and fennel seeds in a mortar using a pestle. Heat 2 tablespoons of olive oil in a small frying pan, add coriander and fennel seeds as well as the peppercorns and fry over a low heat for 1 minute or until fragrant. Remove from heat and leave to cool. Combine cooled oil mixture with remaining oil and add chilli flakes.

Place 2 sprigs rosemary, 1 sprig thyme, 1 strip orange rind and 1 tablespoon balsamic vinegar in the base of a sterilised 2-litre jar. Top with one-third of the olives, then repeat twice with remaining herbs, orange rind, balsamic vinegar and olives. Pour over olive oil mixture to cover.

Refrigerate for at least 1 day before serving to allow flavours to develop. Marinated olives will keep in the refrigerator for up to 1 month in a sterilised jar.

NOTE: To sterilise containers, wash them in hot, soapy water then place them on a baking tray in a 120°C oven for 25-30 minutes. This will prevent harmful bacteria from developing.

FILLS ONE 2-LITRE JAR

1 tablespoon coriander seeds

2 teaspoons fennel seeds

2-2$\frac{1}{2}$ cups extra virgin olive oil

6 black peppercorns

$\frac{1}{2}$ teaspoon chilli flakes

6 large sprigs rosemary

3 large sprigs thyme

3 large strips orange rind

$\frac{1}{4}$ cup aged balsamic vinegar

1 kg mixed olives (including Kalamata, small black olives such as Ligurian, and green olives such as picholine or Sicilian), rinsed well and drained

Stephanie Alexander's
Pickled sardines with chilli

20 fresh sardines

3 tablespoons sea salt

1 cup high-quality red-wine
vinegar

2 cups (approximately)
extra virgin olive oil

several stalks dried oregano

½ cup roughly chopped
flat-leaf parsley

4 cloves garlic, sliced

1-2 fresh chillies
(according to taste),
sliced

Wash sardines and leave them in the refrigerator for 24 hours – this will make them easier to handle.

Using scissors, cut off heads diagonally just under gills and pull out the backbones. The guts will come away with the head. Place sardines in a baking dish, sprinkle generously with sea salt and leave for 2 hours.

Rinse off salt, cover fish with red-wine vinegar and leave for another 2 hours, which cures the flesh and adds flavour. Drain fish thoroughly and pat dry with paper towel.

Put some oil in a clean, sterilised storage container (preferably glass) followed by a layer of sardine fillets. Sprinkle over a little dried oregano, parsley, garlic and chilli. Add more olive oil. Continue to layer fillets and flavourings until you run out of fillets. Then cover completely with olive oil.

Keep in the refrigerator. They can be eaten within a day but are much better after a week or two, and will last in the refrigerator for up to 1 year.

Serve on toasted or grilled bread as an appetiser.

NOTE: To sterilise containers, wash them in hot, soapy water then place them on a baking tray in a 120°C oven for 25-30 minutes. This will prevent harmful bacteria from developing.

MAKES 20 SARDINES

Stephanie has estimated quantities for 20 whole sardines, but the pickle keeps for up to a year so the quantities could easily be doubled or trebled.

Marinate meat in the refrigerator covered with plastic film for at least 2 hours, or overnight if possible. Most fish and seafood should be marinated for no more than 10–20 minutes, but octopus and squid can be marinated for up to 12 hours before cooking. Here, I've given guidelines for my favourite marinades.

Lamb marinade

Dry-roast some coriander and cumin seeds in a small frying pan over a high heat for 30 seconds or until fragrant. Place in a mortar and grind with a pestle, then add chopped fresh oregano, sweet and hot paprika, lemon juice and a good splash of olive oil. Stir to combine and season with sea salt and freshly ground black pepper.

Beef marinade

Process some chopped garlic, chopped anchovy fillets, chopped rosemary, a good splash of balsamic vinegar and olive oil and some red wine or port in a food processor until combined. Season with freshly ground black pepper. This marinade also works well with lamb.

Seafood marinade

Whisk together a good splash of olive oil and the juice and finely grated rind of a lemon, then add some torn basil, finely chopped preserved lemon rind, chopped fresh chilli and garlic and stir to combine. Season with freshly ground black pepper.

Pork marinade

Crush some fennel seeds, garlic and salt with a mortar and pestle until a paste forms. Add chopped thyme and sage and a good splash of olive oil and aged red-wine vinegar and stir to combine. Season with freshly ground black pepper. This marinade also works well with chicken.

Poultry marinade

Process some finely grated lemon rind, a chopped red onion, some sweet paprika, chopped fresh chilli and garlic with a good splash of aged red-wine vinegar and olive oil in a food processor until smooth and well combined. Season to taste with sea salt and freshly ground black pepper.

Truffles, eggs and mayonnaise

Truffles

We revel in Revel, a small village in the south-west of France, one of the few to still have a flourishing produce market at its heart. Occupying an ancient, carousel-shaped building in the town centre, the market is an enchanting setting for local foods and I dream of a time when produce is sold this way in *every* town and city in Australia. Whilst buying cheeses, bread, pâtés, terrines and meats in Revel for a Christmas feast, we were on the lookout for truffles. The French supplies had vanished quickly but there were rumours of Chinese truffles at a nearby charcuterie. We were warned about these imported imposters; they were apparently not as powerful as the French truffles. Indeed, they were hardly truffles at all. But at half the price, we were willing to experiment. We bought our small Chinese stash and returned to the chateau where we were staying to make pasta.

There was one surviving French truffle in that splendid chateau - enthroned in a larder built into a massive tower that had provided the chateau's first line of defence in the fourteenth century. The setting seemed appropriate for such a precious object. There it was, all but glowing in the gloom, in a jar of eggs. Our host had placed it there the previous week so it would permeate the eggs for his breakfasts.

It's hard to imagine a more appetising combination than hunger and the aroma of truffle. We boiled pasta, tossed it in olive oil, grated the Chinese truffles and served it with green salad and vinaigrette.

The next morning our host took the eggs from the tower pantry, scrambled them in olive oil and grated his sole remaining French truffle over the top. It was

a great sacrifice. And it was superb.

A confession is warranted here: I don't think I could tell the difference between a French and a Chinese truffle or, for that matter, between a French and an Australian truffle.

In Italy, truffle-hunters use dogs rather than pigs. I was faintly alarmed when a Tuscan truffler once forbade me to wash the extremely expensive truffles he'd sold us. After all, the dogs that dig them up slobber all over them and the truffles are still covered in dirt when they reach the markets. But, eager to observe tradition, I followed his orders and tried cleaning a truffle with a dry toothbrush instead of washing it. That didn't work, and I would have needed floss for the curves. There still seemed to be more dirt than truffle after grating it.

I was disobedient and used water with the next truffle and was astonished at the amount of dirt hidden within its curves; much of the truffle was dirt in disguise. That night I grated my clean truffle over fresh linguine tossed in olive oil, and even now I still remember its unique, expensive ponginess permeating both the food and the apartment.

Eggs

Rule number one is also rule number two, three and four: eat only fresh organic or biodynamic eggs. By all means keep them in the fridge, but you'll need them at room temperature when making mayonnaise. When you break the egg into a bowl, the yolk should stand up, plump and round, not be broken or flattened. The whites must not be watery.

Mayonnaise

Why is the mayonnaise sold in shops white? Real mayonnaise has egg yolk in it. Will someone explain to me why it isn't yellow?

There are variations on mayonnaise in many cookbooks. But if there's just one thing I'd like you to try from this book, it's homemade mayonnaise. It's the simplest thing in the world to make, and if you do it yourself, you'll know that the oil, eggs and seasoning are of the highest quality and nutritional value.

Although I try only to make enough for one meal at a time, mayonnaise keeps for a week in an airtight container or a bowl covered with plastic film in the fridge. As long as you use fresh eggs at room temperature, it should be easy to get it to thicken.

Some say extra virgin olive oil is too rich for mayonnaise. I firmly disagree. But don't eat too much mayonnaise at once, as the richness can creep up on you and make you feel ill if you overdo it.

Scrambled eggs
with olive oil

This is one of the simplest ways to taste the flavour of extra virgin olive oil. Scrambled eggs and olive oil seriously go together. Serving parsley with eggs is part of my obsession with adding more vitamins to every meal, but there's another reason. I grow parsley from seeds from my mother's garden, and every time I use it, it reminds me of her.

Beat eggs lightly in a cup. Warm oil in a frying pan over a low heat, then add eggs and scramble to the consistency you prefer. Serve 'on the side' or over toast, pour over more olive oil and sprinkle with parsley.

SERVES 1

2 eggs
1 tablespoon olive oil, plus extra to serve
handful chopped flat-leaf parsley

Damien Pignolet's
Salade frisée lardons

300 g pickled pork belly or
smoked bacon

150 ml extra virgin olive oil

6 × ½ cm thick slices light
sourdough bread

1 clove garlic, bruised with
the flat of a knife

1.5 litres water acidulated
with 1 teaspoon vinegar

6 eggs

bowl of iced water

200 g frisée lettuce, washed
and thoroughly dried

Vinaigrette

3 spring onions,
finely sliced

3 tablespoons extra virgin
olive oil

1 tablespoon walnut oil

1 tablespoon red-wine
vinegar

sea salt and freshly ground
black pepper

If using pickled pork belly, simmer it in a saucepan of water for 30 minutes, then drain. Cut pork belly or bacon into lardons about 1 cm × 3 cm in size. Heat a teaspoon of the olive oil in a small frying pan and fry lardons until slightly crisp. Drain on paper towel and keep warm in a very low oven (around 120°C).

To make croutons, cut 5 cm circles out of bread slices and lightly shallow-fry them in the remaining olive oil. Drain on paper towel and then rub with garlic clove.

In a large saucepan, bring acidulated water to the boil and poach eggs so that yolks are still soft and runny; this should take about 2½ minutes. Remove with a slotted spoon and plunge into iced water. Drain on a clean tea towel.

Make vinaigrette by whisking all ingredients together.

Place a poached egg on each crouton and put it in the centre of a plate. Toss frisée lettuce and lardons with vinaigrette and divide among 6 plates, arranging salad around each egg, and serve immediately.

SERVES 6

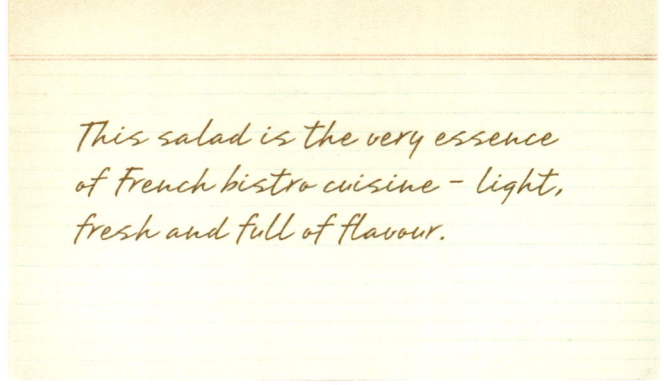

This salad is the very essence of French bistro cuisine – light, fresh and full of flavour.

Traditional mayonnaise

3 egg yolks

2 teaspoons Dijon mustard

200 ml extra virgin olive oil

100 ml sunflower oil

juice of ½–1 lemon

sea salt and freshly ground
black pepper

Place egg yolks and mustard in a bowl and stir to combine. Combine oils and slowly add them to egg yolk mixture, drop by drop at first, whisking to emulsify, then pour them in a thin, steady stream into the bowl, whisking continuously until mayonnaise is thick and well combined. Add lemon juice to taste and whisk until incorporated, then season with salt and pepper.

VARIATIONS: For tarragon mayonnaise, add 2 tablespoons chopped tarragon, 1 clove finely chopped garlic and 1 tablespoon tarragon vinegar. For roast capsicum mayonnaise, roast, peel, seed and chop 1 red capsicum (pepper) (see page 79 for detailed instructions on how to do this), then blend it with the mayonnaise and a large pinch of smoked or sweet paprika in a food processor.

MAKES ABOUT 1½ CUPS

Tartare sauce

1 tablespoon finely chopped
cornichons

1 tablespoon salted capers,
rinsed and finely chopped

1 tablespoon finely chopped
celery

2 tablespoons finely chopped
flat-leaf parsley

1 small clove garlic, finely
chopped

1 tablespoon crème fraîche or
sour cream

1 cup traditional mayonnaise
(see above)

Add cornichons, capers, celery, parsley, garlic and crème fraîche to mayonnaise and stir to combine. This sauce will keep in the refrigerator for up to 3 days, closely covered with plastic film or in an airtight container.

MAKES ABOUT 1½ CUPS

Aïoli

Crush garlic with ½ teaspoon salt in a mortar using a pestle until
a smooth paste forms. Transfer garlic paste to a bowl, add egg yolks
and stir to combine. Slowly add olive oil, drop by drop at first, whisking
to emulsify, then in a thin, steady stream, whisking continuously until
aïoli is thick and well combined. Season with salt and pepper. Aïoli will
keep in the refrigerator for up to 3 days, closely covered with plastic film
or in an airtight container.

MAKES ABOUT 2 CUPS

3-4 large cloves garlic, chopped
sea salt
3 egg yolks
300 ml extra virgin olive oil
freshly ground black pepper

Saffron and lime aïoli

Soak saffron threads in boiling water for 10 minutes. Crush garlic
and add it with the saffron mixture to egg yolks and stir to combine.
Slowly add olive oil, drop by drop at first, whisking to emulsify, then
in a thin, steady stream, whisking continuously until aïoli is thick
and well combined. Season with salt and pepper, then add lime juice
to taste and stir to combine. This aïoli will keep in the refrigerator for
up to 3 days, closely covered with plastic film or in an airtight container.

MAKES ABOUT 2 CUPS

½ teaspoon saffron threads
2 tablespoons boiling water
1 clove garlic
3 egg yolks
300 ml extra virgin olive oil
sea salt and freshly ground
    black pepper
1-2 tablespoons lime juice

Winter soups

We make soup all the time, not just for meals but for afternoon snacks. But it's not a good idea to have big pots that linger too long on the stove, as leaving food at room temperature or reheating it over and over encourages harmful bacteria to grow. It's better to make smaller batches every other day.

The soups you make will depend on the ingredients available. But I always start by heating olive oil in the pan and sautéing chopped onions, and finish off with different herbs, pesto, tapenades, gremolata and/or olive oil. Gremolata is finely chopped lemon rind, fresh garlic and flat-leaf parsley. Use a mezzaluna (a double-handled, crescent-shaped knife) to chop it all together - the finer the better. Store any leftovers in a jar and top with olive oil; it is delicious stirred through pasta or spread on a sandwich.

A favourite of mine is ribollita, one of Italy's most celebrated soups. It's made throughout Tuscany during the olive harvest, and local trattorias compete on the strength of this dish. It is served with *olio nuovo*, the new season's unfiltered oil.

A food associated with the cold season, ribollita is essentially potato, carrot, white beans, Tuscan bread and cavolo nero, the famous long-leafed cabbage. This cabbage needs to be well cooked when it is mature, although the young leaves need less cooking. It is very easy to grow. My friend Fiorenza from Arezzo told me the secrets of her delicious ribollita. Her strict instructions included 'no tomato, basil or zucchini. They are summer foods!'

Holly Davis's
Ribollita

Soak dried cannellini beans overnight in tepid water to which you
have added a squeeze of lemon juice (this makes them more digestible).
Rinse well, place in a saucepan, cover with cold water and bring to
a simmer. Remove any scum as it rises to the surface and simmer for
about 40 minutes or until just tender. Leave beans in cooking water
and set aside.

Place a large, heavy-based stockpot over a low-medium heat.
Add olive oil and onion and sauté until onion is translucent and
beginning to brown (approximately 5 minutes). Add leek and allow
to soften. Add garlic and herbs and cook gently for a minute, then add
carrot, celery and tomato and stir to combine. Pour in cannellini beans
and enough stock to cover well. Season with salt, cover, and simmer
gently over a low heat for approximately 1 hour. Remove lid and add
cavolo nero or cabbage and zucchini. Cook until these are just tender,
then taste and season again if required. Add black pepper and remove
from heat.

Pour soup into warmed bowls and top with bread and parsley.
Drizzle extra virgin olive oil over top and serve.

SERVES 12

*Holly Davis uses an array of
vegetables in her contemporary
interpretation of the classic
ribollita. This recipe makes
enough to feed at least 12 people.*

400 g dried cannellini
    beans *or* 1 × 400 g
    tin cannellini beans,
    drained
squeeze of lemon juice
$\frac{1}{4}$ cup extra virgin olive
    oil, plus extra to serve
2 red onions, finely diced
2 leeks, white part only,
    washed and finely sliced
6 cloves garlic, crushed and
    roughly chopped
1 teaspoon chopped
    rosemary
$\frac{1}{2}$ teaspoon dried oregano
2 carrots, diced
2 stalks young celery, diced
6 ripe roma tomatoes,
    blanched, peeled, seeded
    and diced or 1 × 400 g tin
    chopped tomatoes
3 litres chicken or
    vegetable stock
coarse sea salt
1 bunch cavolo nero
    or $\frac{1}{4}$ Savoy cabbage,
    finely sliced
2 yellow or green zucchinis
    (courgettes), finely diced
coarsely ground black
    pepper
$\frac{1}{2}$ loaf ciabatta, torn into
    rough chunks
handful of chopped flat-
    leaf parsley

1 onion, diced

2 stalks celery, diced

1 small bulb fennel, diced

1 small carrot, diced

1 bulb garlic, chopped

1 leek, thinly sliced

2 golden shallots, thinly
    sliced

small piece fresh ginger,
    thinly sliced

50 ml extra virgin olive oil

250 g lobster heads,
    chopped into 4 cm dice

250 g prawn shells,
    chopped into 4 cm dice

1.5 kg mixed fish bones and
    heads, diced

3 large tomatoes,
    roughly chopped

50 g tomato paste

2 sprigs each thyme,
    marjoram and oregano

5 stalks basil

5 stalks parsley

1 stalk coriander

1 teaspoon sea salt

1/4 teaspoon cardamom

1 teaspoon coriander seeds

1 teaspoon fennel seeds

3 whole star anise

1/4 teaspoon black
    peppercorns

1 teaspoon cayenne pepper

pinch saffron threads

zest of 1/4 orange

25 ml pastis

1.25 litres white wine

Tony Bilson's
Bouillabaisse stock

Place vegetables, ginger and olive oil in a large stockpot and cook until softened. Add lobster heads, prawn shells and fish bones and heads, sauté over a low heat for 5 minutes, then add tomato and tomato paste. Add herbs, spices and orange zest, then the pastis, and simmer until reduced by a third. Pour in wine and 2.5 litres water, bring to the boil and simmer for 1 hour, skimming any scum from the surface. Blend and strain through a fine sieve.

To make a bouillabaisse, use this stock to poach fish, and serve with rouille (see page 83) and croutons made from thinly sliced bread, brushed on both sides with extra virgin olive oil and baked for 5–10 minutes until golden brown.

NOTE: The best fish to use for this stock is a mixture of snapper, john dory, whiting, red mullet, flathead and rock cod. Ask your fishmonger to save heads, shells and bones for you, or buy the whole fish and use the flesh in the final bouillabaisse.

MAKES 5 LITRES

The varieties of fish and shellfish are pivotal to the flavour, as is the olive oil. Making stock may seem difficult at first, but once learnt it will add zest to your life (and years!).

White bean soup

This hearty soup makes a welcome regular appearance on our table in winter. There is something so comforting about its rustic flavours and the inviting aroma of the olive oil as it hits the hot soup. Of course, it helps when you start with homemade chicken stock made from your own produce. Although I generally use cannellini beans, as I like their nutty flavour and creamy texture, other dried beans like borlotti or black-eye beans can also be used.

Soak beans overnight in a large bowl of cold water. Rinse and drain, then place in a large saucepan of water along with bay leaf and thyme and bring to the boil. Reduce the heat to low and simmer for 45 minutes or until tender. Drain and set aside.

Heat olive oil in a stockpot, then add onion, pancetta, carrot and celery and sauté over a low-medium heat for 15 minutes or until softened. Add stock, potato and garlic and bring to the boil. Reduce heat to low and cook for 20 minutes or until vegetables are tender. Add drained beans and tomato paste and cook for another 10 minutes.

Season with salt and pepper, stir in lots of chopped fresh herbs and serve drizzled generously with extra virgin olive oil.

SERVES 4

200 g dried cannellini beans
1 fresh bay leaf
1 sprig thyme
2 tablespoons extra virgin olive oil, plus extra to serve
2 onions, finely chopped
4 slices pancetta or rashers bacon, finely chopped
2 carrots, finely chopped
2 stalks celery, finely chopped
1 litre chicken stock
2 potatoes, diced
1 clove garlic, finely chopped
1 tablespoon tomato paste
sea salt and freshly ground black pepper
handful of chopped fresh herbs

4 lamb shanks

sea salt and freshly ground
    black pepper

130 ml extra virgin olive oil

2 cloves garlic

1 cinnamon stick

1 bay leaf

1 leek, washed and
    halved lengthwise

few sprigs thyme

2 litres (approximately)
    chicken stock

1 large onion, finely diced

2 cloves garlic, finely
    chopped

1 teaspoon ground cumin

1 teaspoon ground turmeric

1 teaspoon ground ginger

1 teaspoon ground
    cinnamon

10 saffron threads, lightly
    roasted and crushed

1 tablespoon honey

1 × 400 g tin chopped
    tomatoes

18 pickling onions, peeled

100 g dried chickpeas,
    soaked overnight and
    cooked or 1 × 400 g tin
    chickpeas, drained

50 ml preserved lemon
    olive oil (see page 93)

60 g flaked almonds, fried
    until golden brown

Greg Malouf's
Tunisian lamb soup with preserved lemon olive oil

Season lamb shanks with salt and pepper. Heat ⅓ cup olive oil in a large heavy-based saucepan over a high heat and brown shanks, turning them so they colour evenly. Lower the heat and drain away any burnt fat. Add garlic, cinnamon, bay leaf, leek and thyme. Pour in stock and bring to the boil. Reduce heat to low and simmer very gently for 2 hours. Skim off any fat and scum that forms on the surface. You may need to top up with a little extra stock, too.

In a medium saucepan, heat remaining olive oil and sauté onion and garlic over a low heat for 5-10 minutes or until they soften. Add spices and cook for another 5 minutes, stirring constantly. Add honey, tomatoes, pickling onions and chickpeas and strain in liquid from lamb shanks. Simmer gently over a low heat for 20-30 minutes.

Remove meat from shanks, discarding bones, fat and sinew. Roughly shred meat and add to soup. Return to a gentle boil over a low heat and taste, adjusting seasoning if necessary.

To serve, ladle soup into bowls, swirl in some preserved lemon olive oil and sprinkle with almonds.

SERVES 6

Lamb shanks are one of my favourite cuts. They need long, slow cooking, but require little attention once they are simmering away. Here, they make a wonderfully fragrant soup with sweet undertones from the honey and cinnamon.

Some special vegetables

The vegetable garden is perhaps my favourite place on earth. As well as providing my ingredients, it gives me peace. Here my big ideas about farming become intimate and domestic, my ambitions for sustainability and quality meet.

The seasons dictate my menus. No broccoli in summer or fresh tomatoes in winter; we eat whatever is in season, depending on how well I planned and planted. The garden is dominated by annual plantings of old-timers - easy-to-grow basics like lettuce, broccoli, cabbage, zucchini, pumpkin, carrot, leek, onion, beetroot, tomatoes and basil. I decorate it with herbs such as dill and coriander, and if there is room to spare I experiment with celeriac, cauliflower, rare potatoes, snow peas, parsnips, turnips, and seeds from friends. Wild mushrooms appear in the hills.

We press our oil in March and April, which coincides with the last of the basil, eggplants, tomatoes, capsicums, zucchini, potatoes, and summer herbs like fennel. And my best friends, beans.

Artichokes

Although they've regained some popularity, globe artichokes present a formidable challenge, both in the cooking and the eating. Even a distinguished chef who was helping us clean some artichokes fresh from the garden admitted, 'I don't bother with them, they're too difficult.'

I disagree - I think they're worth a lot of bother. For a start, they're spectacular in appearance. They belong to the Cynara thistle family and come in my favourite colours, purple and green. Even if you don't like eating artichokes, try placing some in a vase in the centre of your table. And those eccentric Europeans eat whole, small artichokes raw. They're as common as carrots in Italy, and when you sample fresh oil you'll often find a plate of thinly sliced raw artichoke to eat with it.

To prepare them, have a large bowl of water with lemon juice in it on hand. Cut the tips off the flower, leaving a few inches of stem - it's very tasty. Pull off the hard outer leaves and gouge out the hairy 'choke' in the centre. Eating an artichoke is much more pleasant once this hairy, inedible centre is removed, but getting it out isn't easy. Using a sharp knife, carefully cut the choke away from the flesh, then scoop it out with a spoon. Place each artichoke in the acidulated water as you finish preparing it; the lemon juice will prevent your artichokes from turning grey.

Aluminium and iron also turn artichokes an unappetising shade of grey, so when cooking them use stainless steel utensils. While they're boiling in plenty of salty water (this will take about 45-60 minutes, depending on size), make mayonnaise, aïoli, or whichever dressing you prefer. Serve the dressing in individual bowls so your guests can double-dip, or simply serve with small bowls of fresh olive oil.

I prefer larger artichokes, since they're easier to eat, and I usually serve one per guest. The trick is to clench the leaf between your teeth and tug (decorously, of course) to release the soft fleshy bits. The process of eating an artichoke creates a considerable amount of detritus - they're a bit like oysters in that regard. There's a lot of packaging for every delicious mouthful. It takes a long time to get to the heart; when you arrive, use a knife and fork for some open-heart surgery. Delicious.

Beans

Home-grown beans have a quality denied purchased beans, which are often has-beens. Beans are enthusiastic plants. They really try to grow, only asking one thing: to be eaten fresh. I once met a woman in France who apologised for picking her beans in the morning when they were intended for dinner. She thought I'd think them stale.

We grow a few different kinds: purple, yellow and green, but my favourite is the alarmingly named snake bean (*Vigna unguiculata*), which is from a different family than the common bean (*Phaseolus vulgaris*). The differences in both appearance and behaviour are obvious when you grow them.

I pick snake beans when they're 24 cm long and thinner than pencils. I cut them into 6 cm strips and drop them into salted boiling water for a maximum of 3 minutes. While they're boiling, I dry-roast a generous cup of pecans or walnuts. I then drain the beans, tip them into a bowl, drizzle fresh olive oil onto them, toss so

all the beans are coated, and sprinkle the nuts and some ground salt over them. They are gone within seconds. The perfect after-school snack when the kitchen is crowded with kids.

Beetroot

I grew up in the grim era of canned, sliced beetroot. It was a principal ingredient in summer and always starred in our hamburgers. Nowadays there are scores of varieties and they are easy to grow.

If you're using big ones, wash them but don't cut into the flesh - just tear off the leafy tops and give these to the chooks or put them in the compost if you don't use them later yourself. Boil the beetroot until it's cooked right through, which will take up to 30 minutes. Rinse in cold water; this will help you slide off the skin. Eat immediately or slice and store in a vinaigrette dressing. They'll last in the fridge for a few days. If using small ones, wash them, cut off their tops and the hairy roots, toss in olive oil, add salt and pepper and bake them whole as a side dish. Before serving, crumble goat's cheese or fetta generously over the beetroot and pour on olive oil. I also like to cut smaller pieces and roast them for risotto, always cooking extra for a salad the following day. At the same time I'll cook sweet potato or pumpkin on another tray.

If you use a wood-fired barbecue, place whole, unpeeled beetroots on the hot grill and let them bake slowly for 2 hours. The smell is fantastic. Serve whole or cut into chunks tossed in olive oil. They'll also keep in the fridge for a few days.

You can eat purple beetroot raw (some people have reported a burning sensation in the throat when eating raw golden beetroot, so approach with caution). Grate with carrot and toss together with vinaigrette. The colour is fantastic and everyone has second helpings.

Carrots

Being a kitchen staple, carrots are not seen as one of the glamour vegetables, but it is their versatility that makes them at once common and special. It would be almost unthinkable to start making a soup or stew without the holy trinity of carrots, onion and celery (referred to in French cuisine as a *mirepoix*). Year-round demand for carrots makes them a permanent fixture on greengrocers' shelves, so we forget that, as a root vegetable, their true season is winter.

Many of us may remember boring boiled carrots, perhaps glazed with honey by more adventurous cooks, sitting alongside the meat and the other two vegetables of our childhood meals. Their natural sweetness makes carrots suited to roasting with olive oil, and Moroccan cooks often pair them with orange blossom water in salads, making a much more exotic offering. Treated like this, I eat them because they're delicious, and not just because they're good for me.

Fennel

Although it is often available in greengrocers, fennel remains largely unfamiliar in the Australian kitchen. Simply braised or chopped into soup or risotto instead of celery, it is wonderful. Better still, leave it raw, slice it and dip it in olive oil as an appetiser or accompaniment to a rich main course.

Pinzimonio (see page 130)

Garlic

We grow and use a lot of garlic. If you're adding it to dips, it's particularly good if you bake it first - slice the top off the bulb, sit it on a piece of foil, pour olive oil over it, sprinkle with salt, wrap it up and bake for 15 minutes. Or lightly boil the bulbs for 2 minutes and slide them out of their skins. This makes them slightly less pungent.

Potatoes

French-style mashed potato with butter and milk is a perfect dish, but there are times when even perfection can be improved. We now serve a new 'traditional' mash with our homemade beef sausages. Cook potatoes with their skins on to retain the potassium and mash potatoes with olive oil instead of butter. Serve with chopped herbs on top. Or bake potatoes in their skins, so that everyone can slice their own open and add the amount of olive oil that suits them. Prick the skins a few times with a fork, then rub them generously with olive oil and sprinkle with salt before baking - this makes the skin deliciously crunchy.

Or cut potatoes into wedges, place them on a tray, brush them with olive oil and sprinkle with chopped sage, thyme or rosemary, either fresh or dried. Bake them in a very hot oven for about 1 hour, adding whole cloves of unpeeled garlic for the last 10 minutes. Garlic is easy to overcook or burn, but adding it at a later stage and leaving the skins on helps prevent this.

For potato salad, steam new potatoes with their skins on, drain and cool to room temperature, cut into pieces and add salt, chopped onion, herbs and olive oil. To be more traditional, toss the potatoes with homemade mayonnaise (made with olive oil, of course) instead of straight olive oil.

Potatoes are perfect with leftover lentil soup. When you make lentil soup, make extra and keep half in the fridge for a lentil and potato dinner the following night.

Reheat the soup, which will have thickened naturally in the fridge overnight, and steam some potatoes - cut in half if big. Chop up a generous cup of flat-leaf parsley. When the potatoes are almost done, toss a bunch of washed, chopped English spinach into the heated lentil soup. The spinach doesn't need to cook, just wilt. Grind in salt and pepper. Put the potatoes on wide bowls or plates and lightly press down on them with a fork. Ladle the soup over the top and pour olive oil over the lot.

Zucchini

Zucchinis are much maligned, but they are actually an incredibly versatile vegetable. You can pick them small and eat them raw; stuff their flowers and deep-fry them; roast, barbecue or grate them; add them to soup; slice and add them to your boiling pasta two minutes before draining. And zucchini slice is a dish any cook, however new, can learn.

Pinzimonio

A selection of vegetables, such as quartered baby fennel, trimmed and scrubbed baby carrots, radishes, pencil leeks, red capsicum (pepper) strips, cucumber batons, celery sticks, broccoli florets, green and butter beans, young broad beans and baby beetroot
extra virgin olive oil to serve
sea salt and freshly ground black pepper

When you really want to celebrate the diversity of raw vegetables, you can't do better than this. Pinzimonio can serve as many as you like — just adjust quantities to suit numbers.

Blanch the broccoli, beans and beetroot and leave the other vegetables raw. Serve with a bowl of your finest extra virgin olive oil mixed with sea salt and freshly ground black pepper for dipping.

Zucchini slice

6 rashers bacon
4 zucchinis (courgettes), grated
1 large onion, chopped
1 cup grated cheddar
1 cup self-raising flour
$\frac{1}{2}$ cup extra virgin olive oil
5 eggs, beaten
pinch ground cumin
$\frac{1}{2}$ teaspoon ground coriander
sea salt and freshly ground black pepper

Preheat oven to 170°C and grease a large baking dish (deep or shallow according to your preference) with olive oil. Chop bacon rashers into 1 cm pieces and fry until cooked. Allow to cool. Mix all ingredients together in bowl, pour into a baking dish and bake for approximately 40 minutes until set and golden. Serve warm with a fresh green salad.

SERVES 4

Serge Dansereau's
Confit of small vegetables

In a large copper or heavy-based saucepan, heat olive oil over a very low heat. Add garlic and hard vegetables (artichokes, onions, potatoes, leeks, fennel, carrots, celery, radishes and turnips) and cook, covered, over a low heat for 15 minutes. Add remaining vegetables except peas, and cook for another 10 minutes over a low heat. Add peas, deglaze pan with balsamic vinegar and remove from heat. Add oregano and butter and mix until butter glazes vegetables. Sprinkle with fleur de sel and serve immediately.

SERVES 4

This is 'one pot' vegetable magic. A vast array of seasonal vegetables, cooked simply and moistened by olive oil (and top-quality butter from grass-fed cows!).

100 ml extra virgin olive oil

4 cloves garlic

2 large globe artichoke hearts, choke removed (see page 122 for instructions), cut in 4 and dipped in lemon juice

4 pickling onions, peeled

8 small new potatoes, washed

4 very young leeks, white part only, washed and root trimmed

1 small bulb fennel, trimmed and quartered

4 baby carrots, peeled or scrubbed

2 celery hearts, trimmed and cut in half

4 small red radishes, trimmed

4 small turnips, peeled

4 green and 4 yellow baby zucchinis (courgettes)

8 asparagus tips, trimmed

4 baby green beans, trimmed

80 g young peas

50 ml aged balsamic vinegar

1 handful oregano, leaves picked

100 g cold butter, diced

2 tablespoons fleur de sel (French sea salt)

Cath Claringbold's
Tunisian carrot salad

1 kg carrots, cut into
   batons
extra virgin olive oil for
   coating
sea salt and freshly ground
   black pepper
large handful pitted
   Kalamata olives, rinsed
   and cut in half
handful roughly chopped
   flat-leaf parsley
handful roughly chopped
   coriander

Harissa
2 red capsicums (peppers)
25 g fresh bird's eye
   chillies, with half the
   seeds removed
2 teaspoons cumin seeds,
   roasted and crushed
1 teaspoon coriander seeds,
   roasted and crushed
4 cloves garlic
100 ml extra virgin olive oil
sea salt

Harissa vinaigrette
4 cloves garlic
sea salt
2 tablespoons harissa
100 ml white-wine vinegar
$\frac{1}{2}$ cup extra virgin olive oil
freshly ground black
   pepper

First make harissa. Cut capsicums into quarters and remove seeds.
Arrange capsicum on a baking tray, skin-side up, and cook under a hot
grill until skins blacken and blister. Place in a plastic bag and leave for
5 minutes - the steam will loosen the skins, making them easier to peel.
Peel capsicums and blend them with the other harissa ingredients in
a food processor or blender to form a smooth paste. Harissa will keep
in the fridge for a week.

Next make harissa vinaigrette. Crush garlic with a pinch of salt
in a mortar using a pestle until very smooth. Add harissa and whisk
in vinegar, then oil, and season with salt and pepper.

Preheat oven to 180°C. Coat carrots with a little olive oil and season
with salt and pepper. Cook in a covered roasting tray in oven for about
45 minutes or until tender. Allow carrots to cool to room temperature.

To serve, toss carrots, olives, parsley, coriander and a generous
amount of harissa vinaigrette together and serve.

SERVES 4-6

*North African food has such
wonderful, robust flavours whilst
being a very healthy cuisine.
It is also perfect for sharing
and works well all year round.*

Sean Moran's
Artichokes with gremolata

Pour olive oil into a lidded, enamelled cast-iron pot into which artichokes will fit snugly. Peel and coarsely smash 4 of the garlic cloves, then add to oil with oregano, sage, thyme and wine. Zest and juice 1 of the lemons and add to pot.

Trim about 3 cm from the top of each artichoke, then cut away (but keep) stalks. Discard a few of the darker outside leaves and tidy up any fibres with a sharp knife, then submerge in olive oil. Carefully peel each stalk, keeping it smooth and as round as possible. Add these to oil and season generously.

Bring pot to the boil over a medium heat, then reduce to a steady simmer until the stalks are just tender; this should take about 25 minutes. Remove pot from heat, remove stalks with a slotted spoon and leave to cool. Return pot to heat and simmer until artichoke hearts are tender (about another 25 minutes). Remove with a slotted spoon and allow to cool. Keep the cooking juices - these become the dressing.

Add a spoonful of olive oil from the top of the artichoke pot to a frying pan and heat over a medium heat. Sauté breadcrumbs until deep golden, then drain on paper towel.

Meanwhile, make gremolata. Remove rind from remaining lemon and mince it with remaining parsley and garlic in a food processor.

When artichokes are cool enough to handle, carefully part centre leaves to reveal the 'choke'. Carefully scoop this out using a teaspoon and discard. Open up the flower and loosely stuff gremolata and crumbs between leaves and in the heart. Stir cooking juices well and check seasoning, then drizzle generously over artichoke hearts and stalks and serve.

SERVES 4-6

1 litre extra virgin olive oil
6 cloves garlic
several oregano leaves, roughly chopped
several sage leaves, roughly chopped
several sprigs thyme, bruised
150 ml dry white wine
2 lemons
4-6 globe artichokes
sea salt and freshly ground black pepper
handful coarse fresh breadcrumbs
2 handfuls chopped flat-leaf parsley

The crunch of the golden breadcrumbs adds a lovely texture to the silky artichokes, simmered till tender in olive oil.

Philip Johnson's
Fennel à la grecque

3 large or 6 baby
   bulbs fennel
1 litre cold water
½ cup extra virgin olive oil
juice of 2 lemons
3 bay leaves
few sprigs thyme
1 teaspoon coriander seeds
few black peppercorns
good pinch sea salt

Trim outside layers from fennel. Cut each bulb into 6-8 wedges, depending on size (if using baby fennel, just cut them in half).

Pour water into a saucepan and add olive oil, lemon juice, bay leaves, thyme, coriander seeds, peppercorns and salt. Bring to the boil, then add fennel. Cover with baking paper and a small plate to keep fennel submerged during cooking. Simmer gently for 10-15 minutes or until tender. Allow to cool in the liquid.

Serve at room temperature with some of the cooking liquid spooned over it. This is perfect with grilled seafood, such as salmon or prawns, or as a side dish.

SERVES 6 AS AN ACCOMPANIMENT

This dish highlights fennel's subtle flavour and texture. The braising makes it soft to eat, and any leftovers work well for salads, soups or sandwiches.

Belinda Jeffery's
New potatoes with olive oil and garlic

1 kg small new potatoes

100 ml extra virgin olive oil

2 cloves garlic, crushed

leaves from 2 large sprigs
   rosemary

sea salt and freshly ground
   black pepper

tiny rosemary sprigs to
   serve (optional)

Scrub potatoes, leaving skins on. Sit them in a single layer in a very large, heavy-based frying pan and add cold water to a depth of 4 mm. Cover pan tightly and bring water to the boil over a high heat. As soon as it boils, reduce heat to very low and let water simmer until it has been completely absorbed. Remove pan from heat and wipe away any condensation from the underside of the lid.

Add olive oil and garlic to pan and give it a good shake so potatoes are really well coated. Sit pan back over a low heat, cover, and cook for 30 minutes, giving the pan a shake regularly, and occasionally wiping condensation from the underside of the lid. (If potatoes don't roll over easily, turn them with a spoon.) Check potatoes - they should be golden on the outside and tender when you pierce one with a fine skewer. If they're not very golden, increase heat a little and cook for a few minutes longer. Add rosemary, salt and pepper, shake pan again and cook for 1 more minute. Tumble them out into a warm bowl, sprinkle the rosemary sprigs on top, if using, and serve straight away.

SERVES 4-6

These potatoes need to be cooked in one layer so that they will form a crisp crust with a soft interior.

Stefano Manfredi's
Roast beetroot and hazelnuts with gorgonzola

100 g hazelnuts

20 small to medium
    beetroots (a mixture
    of the usual red and
    unusual golden beets
    is a good idea)

extra virgin olive oil for
    sprinkling

sea salt and freshly ground
    black pepper

150 g gorgonzola, broken
    into chunks

Preheat oven to 180°C. Roast hazelnuts for about 8 minutes, taking care not to let them burn. Remove from oven and crush lightly in a mortar using a pestle.

Trim stem and beard from beetroots. Scrub well with a soft brush under cold water. Place in some foil and sprinkle with a little olive oil, salt and pepper. Seal package and roast in the oven until tender (this will take upwards of 15 minutes, depending on their size). Open foil and allow to cool before peeling and quartering each one. Place quartered beets on four individual ceramic plates, or one large heatproof serving plate, and sprinkle with a little extra virgin olive oil, salt and pepper.

Scatter gorgonzola chunks over beets. Place under a hot grill for 1 minute until cheese has melted. Scatter crushed hazelnuts on top and serve.

SERVES 4

The sweetness of the beetroot is a good foil to the salty, savoury gorgonzola, while the hazelnuts provide texture and flavour. This recipe needs a peppery extra virgin olive oil.

Salads as sides or meals

It's easy to build a whole meal around a salad. Fresh vegetables from the garden, some meat, fish, eggs, cheese or pulses and a zingy dressing, served with a glass of chilled wine and some crusty bread, and in no time you have a meal that's both refreshing and healthy. The vitamins in the vegetables help you absorb nutrients from the rest of your food, so try to have some salad every day. Some of the salads here can be served as an accompaniment to meals, while others are a meal in themselves.

Caprese salad

Caprese salad (Insalata Caprese)

This simple salad relies on the freshness and integrity of the tomatoes, basil and mozzarella.

Alternately layer slices of tomato and mozzarella on a large plate or serving dish. Scatter with basil leaves, then season with salt and pepper. Drizzle with olive oil immediately before serving.

SERVES 4

2 cored ox-heart (beef)
    tomatoes or 4 vine-ripened
    tomatoes, sliced widthwise
500 g buffalo mozzarella,
    gently torn
$\frac{1}{3}$ cup small basil leaves
sea salt and freshly ground
    black pepper
$\frac{1}{4}$ cup extra virgin olive oil

Panzanella

The ingenious Tuscans created this vibrant salad as a way of using their stale bread.

Cut capsicums into quarters and remove seeds. Arrange capsicum on a baking tray, skin-side up, and roast under a hot grill until their skins blacken and blister. Place in a plastic bag and leave for 5 minutes - the steam helps to loosen the skins, making them easier to peel. Peel capsicum and slice thinly.

Cut cucumbers into bite-sized pieces. Tear ciabatta into bite-sized pieces. Combine capsicums and their juices, cucumber, tomato, garlic, shallot, olive oil and vinegar in a large bowl. Season with salt and pepper and toss to combine. Leave to stand at room temperature for 30 minutes to allow flavours to meld.

Just before serving, add bread and basil and toss to combine.

SERVES 6

3 red capsicums (peppers)
1 yellow capsicum (pepper)
2 Lebanese cucumbers
6 x 2 cm thick slices day-old
    ciabatta, crusts removed
6 roma tomatoes, seeded
    and chopped
1 clove garlic, finely chopped
1 golden shallot, finely chopped
$\frac{1}{2}$ cup extra virgin olive oil
2 tablespoons red-wine vinegar
sea salt and freshly ground
    black pepper
$\frac{1}{2}$ cup small basil leaves, torn

Damien Pignolet's
Chicken salad with coddled egg vinaigrette

4-5 skinless, boneless
   chicken breasts

2 bunches medium-
   thick asparagus, bases
   trimmed

3 heads witlof, outer layer
   of leaves removed

$\frac{1}{4}$ cup chopped blanched
   almonds or whole pine
   nuts, dry-roasted until
   golden

2 punnets mustard cress
   or generous handful
   small watercress sprigs,
   washed and snipped

Poaching stock

2 golden shallots,
   thinly sliced

1 carrot, diced

1 stalk celery, diced

3 sprigs thyme

1 bay leaf

150 ml dry vermouth or
   dry white wine

about 1 litre cold water

6 cracked black
   peppercorns

2-3 teaspoons sea salt

Take chicken breasts out of fridge 30 minutes before cooking.

Select a sauté pan or wide pan which has a tight-fitting lid and will accommodate the breasts in one layer without them being crammed into the pan. Put poaching stock ingredients into the pan and bring slowly to the boil. Simmer for 30 minutes, skimming off any scum that rises to the surface. Taste and adjust seasoning - it should be quite highly seasoned.

Strain resulting broth, rinse out pan and pour broth back into it. Return to a rapid boil. Add chicken breasts; they must be submerged, so have the kettle boiling to top up if needed. Put on lid and turn off heat. (Take pan off stove completely if cooking with electricity.) Leave untouched for 10 minutes.

Transfer chicken breasts to a plate, cover lightly with plastic film and leave for 15 minutes to rest and complete the cooking. (Reserve broth, as it can be used as a soup base.)

Diagonally slice off asparagus tips in lengths of about 3-4 cm, then continue slicing stalks in 2 cm lengths. Cook for 2-3 minutes in a saucepan of salted boiling water (they should remain firm). Drain and refresh under cold running water until cold. Drain and transfer to a plate.

This is a perfect summer lunch; follow it with cheese and fresh fruit. The quality of the chicken makes all the difference, so select free-range and organic.

Trim roots from witlof, then cut each into sixths lengthwise.

To make vinaigrette, place each egg on a board and crack with a sharp knife, then open over a large bowl so the yolk can run into it. Use a teaspoon to scoop out any remaining firmer yolk. Finely chop whites.

Combine mustard, salt and plenty of white pepper with the egg yolks. Slowly whisk in olive oil to achieve a thickened texture, as if making a mayonnaise. Gradually add vinegar until it tastes fresh but not too sharp. Add egg whites and parsley.

Carve chicken breasts into 1 cm slices widthwise and add to vinaigrette, along with witlof and asparagus stalks, keeping tips for a finishing touch. Toss gently to coat the ingredients with the vinaigrette.

Distribute chicken, asparagus and witlof among 6 large plates. Arrange asparagus tips on top then scatter with nuts and cress and serve.

SERVES 6

Vinaigrette

2 eggs, boiled for 3 minutes and then refreshed in cold water

1 heaped teaspoon Dijon mustard

$^1/_4$ teaspoon sea salt

freshly ground white pepper

$^1/_2$ cup extra virgin olive oil

1-2 tablespoons good-quality white-wine vinegar

2 tablespoons finely chopped flat-leaf parsley

Janni Kyritsis'
Pan-fried vegetables with skordalia salad and zucchini-flower fritters

3 eggplants (aubergines), trimmed and cut lengthwise into 5 mm thick slices
6 zucchinis (courgettes), trimmed and cut lengthwise into 5 mm thick slices
6 bulbs baby fennel, trimmed and cut into 6 wedges
sea salt and freshly ground black pepper
extra virgin olive oil for shallow-frying

Skordalia salad
1/4 cup extra virgin olive oil
125 g blanched almonds
1 large slice sourdough bread, crusts removed, cut into 4 mm cubes
1 cup roughly chopped flat-leaf parsley
1/2 cup chopped garlic chives
juice and finely grated rind of 1 lemon
sea salt and freshly ground black pepper

Zucchini-flower fritters
200 ml pale beer
2 teaspoons each sea salt and freshly ground white pepper
100 g plain flour, sifted
12 zucchini (courgette) flowers, gently opened

For skordalia salad, heat olive oil in a small frying pan, add almonds and stir over a low heat until golden. Remove with a slotted spoon and drain on paper towel. Chop coarsely with a large, sharp knife. Add bread to pan and fry until crisp, stirring constantly, then drain on paper towel. Just before serving, place croutons, almonds and remaining skordalia ingredients in a bowl, season with salt and pepper and toss well.

Season eggplant, zucchini and fennel with salt and pepper, stand for 30 minutes, then pat dry with paper towel. Heat 5 mm oil in a large, heavy-based frying pan and cook vegetables, in batches, over a medium-high heat until tender and golden, adding more oil if necessary. Drain on paper towel, reserving pan and remaining oil.

To make fritters, combine beer, salt and pepper in a bowl and sieve flour over beer, whisking until just combined. Add olive oil to pan to a depth of 2 cm and heat over a medium heat until a drop of water sizzles when dropped in. Dip zucchini flowers in batter, drain off any excess, and fry in batches until golden and crisp. Drain on paper towel.

Serve vegetables with fritters, and pass salad around separately.

SERVES 6-8

This makes a wonderful vegetarian lunch — the different textures of the vegetables and crunchy fritters are very satisfying. Skordalia is usually a dip, but here the same ingredients are used in a salad.

24 yellow beans, trimmed

24 green beans, trimmed

½ cup red-wine vinegar

1 clove garlic, chopped

2 golden shallots, chopped

100 ml walnut oil

120 ml extra virgin olive oil

sea salt and freshly ground
    black pepper

100 g pecans

150 g baby spinach

Duck confit

4 duck marylands,
    knuckles chopped off

rind of 1 orange, finely
    grated

rind of 1 lemon, finely
    grated

1 bay leaf

pinch crushed black
    peppercorns

100 g sea salt

2 crushed juniper berries

1 litre extra virgin olive oil

Serge Dansereau's
Bean salad with duck confit

To make confit, wash duck and pat dry with paper towel. In a bowl, combine orange and lemon rind, bay leaf, black pepper, sea salt and juniper berries and coat duck with the mixture. Marinate duck in an ovenproof dish (with lid on) in the refrigerator for 4 hours.

Preheat oven to 140°C. Take duck from marinade, rinse under cold water, then pat dry with paper towel. Discard marinade and wash dish. Return duck to clean dish and cover with olive oil.

Cook in the oven for 2 hours or until meat is falling off bones. Remove from oven and cool in the oil. Once cooled, remove duck from dish and discard skin and bones, then return meat to oil.

Cook beans in salted boiling water until tender (about 5–8 minutes). Remove and plunge into cold water, then halve lengthwise.

To make dressing, heat vinegar, garlic and shallots in a small saucepan over a high heat and reduce by a quarter. Remove from heat and cool. Once cooled, whisk in walnut oil and 100 ml of olive oil. Season with salt and pepper.

Preheat oven to 150°C and roast pecans for about 10 minutes, taking care not to burn them. Gently warm up confit by placing it in a frying pan over a medium heat, with a little of the olive oil it is stored in, for 3 minutes on each side.

Heat remaining tablespoon of olive oil in a frying pan, add spinach and quickly toss until just wilted. Remove and place in a salad bowl with beans, duck confit, pecans and dressing. Toss salad and arrange on serving plates.

SERVES 4

This recipe should be started ahead of time, as the duck confit needs 4 hours to marinate. It still meets my 10-minute rule — except it's 10 minutes here and there. It's a very wholesome dish.

8 fresh (live) yabbies

150 ml white wine

1/2 onion, chopped

1 stalk celery, sliced

2 bay leaves

3 black peppercorns

5 coriander seeds

bowl of iced water

1 smoked rainbow trout

2 ripe avocados

juice of 1 lemon

2 ruby grapefruit, peeled
    and segmented

1/2 bunch chives, finely
    chopped

1/2 bunch chervil, leaves
    picked

160 g mixed salad leaves

extra virgin olive oil for
    drizzling

Vinaigrette

2 golden shallots, finely
    sliced

1 clove garlic, finely
    chopped

2 tablespoons verjuice

2 teaspoons sherry vinegar

100 ml extra virgin olive oil

pinch sugar

sea salt and freshly ground
    black pepper

Janet Jeffs'
Smoked rainbow trout
and yabby tail salad

Place yabbies in freezer for 1 hour before cooking to make them go to sleep. Place wine, 1 litre water, onion, celery, bay leaves and spices in a large saucepan and bring to the boil. Add yabbies in two batches and cook for 5 minutes or until they turn a vibrant red colour. Remove from liquid and place in a bowl of iced water to stop cooking. If you prefer your yabbies peeled, extract tails, discarding shells, heads, legs and claws. Set tails aside.

Remove skin and break up flesh of trout, removing all bones

Cut avocados in half, remove stones and peel off skin. Cut in half again and brush with lemon juice to prevent discolouration. Divide among four plates.

For vinaigrette, combine shallots, garlic, verjuice and vinegar in a bowl. Drizzle in olive oil slowly while whisking constantly, until combined. Add sugar, salt and pepper and set aside.

Place yabby tails, trout, grapefruit, herbs and salad leaves in a bowl. Add vinaigrette and toss until combined. Arrange on plates over avocados, drizzle with olive oil and serve.

SERVES 4

This is a great salad with delicately contrasting flavours. The dressing adds complexity to the dish, so it's especially important that the olive oil you use is of high quality.

152

Holly Davis's
Spring scallop salad

1 handful sugar snap peas,
strings removed

bowl of iced water

3 large handfuls broad
beans, shelled

20 raw scallops with
corals intact

1 tablespoon raw sesame
oil (not toasted)

1 bunch watercress,
washed and sprigs
picked

1 packet sunflower sprouts
(optional)

sea salt

coarsely ground black
pepper

2 tablespoons extra virgin
olive oil

rind of 1 lemon,
finely grated

1 teaspoon naturally
fermented white-wine
vinegar

Bring a saucepan of salted water to a rolling boil. Quickly blanch peas and refresh in a bowl of iced water, then drain and set aside.

Blanch broad beans for 7-10 minutes until just tender, then refresh in iced water and drain. Peel broad beans a second time to release the tender, bright green beans beneath, discard skins and set beans aside with peas.

Toss scallops in the sesame oil. Heat a heavy-based skillet, chargrill pan or frying pan over a high heat until very hot. Sear scallops for 30 seconds on each side and remove from pan to cool.

Gently toss watercress and sunflower sprouts, if using, together in a salad bowl. Top with peas, broad beans and scallops. Season with salt and pepper. Pour over olive oil with lemon rind and vinegar and serve.

SERVES 4-6

The olive oil with lemon zest complements this dish – the citrussy taste suits the Asian flavours perfectly. Take care only to use the yellow rind of the lemon, as the pith is bitter.

Risotto, pasta and polenta

In much of my home cooking, I take inspiration from the simplicity and style of the Italian kitchen. I am never without a ready supply of good-quality risotto rice (I like to use arborio), pasta and polenta, and these pantry staples ensure that I can have a wonderful meal on the table in less time than it would take to drive to get take-away. I supplement these with my own garden-grown produce and extra virgin olive oil.

While risotto, pasta and polenta have now become interchangeable as the carbohydrate component of meals on tables across Italy, only a few generations ago you could tell which region you were in by which one of these you were served.

Risotto

Risotto was primarily restricted to the north and centre of Italy, close to the rice-producing areas. In Australia we are more familiar with the stickier style of risotto, where the liquid is mostly absorbed by the rice, and this is preferred in Piedmont, Emilia-Romagna and Lombardy, whereas the Venetians favour a more liquid, soupier style.

Pasta

Pasta, especially in its dried forms, was traditionally the food of the south. The variety of shapes available is as endless as the range of sauces you can make to go with it, and neither fresh nor dried is better than the other; the choice really depends on how you want to serve it. As a general rule, which can be broken, dried pasta is better suited to olive oil and vegetable-based sauces, while fresh pasta is best served with sauces based on butter or cream.

Polenta

Traditionally, polenta was the key source of sustenance for the Veneto, Friuli and Lombardy regions, where it was served as a first or second course, side dish or entrée. Grilled polenta can be served with a wonderful variety of toppings, such as prosciutto, fig and gorgonzola drizzled with olive oil and scattered with a little finely sliced mint; or pesto, mozzarella and cherry tomatoes. It is also good with tapenade and many of the sauces in this book. See page 167 for a polenta recipe you can adapt to your own taste.

Basic risotto

Apart from making meals go further when hungry people suddenly appear, risotto is the perfect comfort food. I usually make a plain risotto and top it with vegetables, my favourites being sweet potato or beetroot. I like risotto to be white with a hint of the beetroot bled into the rice. To achieve this, make sure you only mix the cooked beetroot in at the last minute. For a totally red risotto that goes really well with fish, use red wine in the stock and mix the cooked beetroot through to begin with.

Heat olive oil in a large saucepan and lightly fry (but don't brown) garlic. Add rice; toss it in oil and garlic and heat through. At this stage you might be concerned that it is too oily, but don't worry. As the rice swells and absorbs water, the oil will be incorporated into the mix. Add verjuice, then stock. Recipes insist you have the stock heated and ready to stir into the risotto a ladleful at a time, but I've had good results with cold stock, even when I've poured it all in at once. However, if you're new to risotto, add stock little by little until it is all absorbed, stirring constantly so the rice doesn't stick. Twenty minutes later, the rice should be cooked but not gluggy. When the risotto reaches your preferred consistency (Phillip likes his runny and I like mine drier), stir in half the parmesan. Place baked vegetables on top. Add the rest of the parmesan and the parsley and serve.

SERVES 2

$\frac{1}{3}$ **cup olive oil**

2 large cloves garlic

1 cup risotto rice (eg arborio)

$\frac{1}{2}$ **cup verjuice**

about 1 litre stock

1 cup grated parmesan

1 cup baked vegetables of
**   your choice**

handful chopped flat-leaf
**   parsley**

Risotto fritters

The 'one cup of rice per couple' rule also allows enough leftover risotto for making fritters the next day. You may find your family prefers the fritters to the risotto.

2 eggs

1 cup leftover risotto (see page 159 for recipe)

handful chopped herbs (eg parsley and basil)

½ cup olive oil

Beat eggs and mix with leftover risotto. This will look quite runny. Add chopped fresh herbs. Pour olive oil into a frying pan over a high heat. Once oil is really hot (the surface will shimmer slightly), drop in tablespoons of risotto mix. Fry one side of your fritters very brown. Flip once and cook lightly on the other side. Drain on paper towel before serving with a dressed, tossed salad.

Tobie Puttock's
Spaghetti with olive oil, breadcrumbs and fresh chilli

Bring a large pot of salted water to the boil. Plunge spaghetti into boiling water and cook according to manufacturer's instructions.

While spaghetti is cooking, heat 2 tablespoons olive oil in a frying pan over a medium heat and fry breadcrumbs for 1-2 minutes, until golden and crisp. Remove and drain on paper towels. Turn heat to low and add remaining olive oil to frying pan along with garlic, chilli, anchovies and parsley stalks. Very gently warm the olive oil over a low heat to infuse the flavours, being careful not to brown garlic or heat oil too much. This should only take a couple of minutes. Remove pan from heat.

Once spaghetti is cooked, drain and add it to frying pan along with parsley leaves, breadcrumbs and parmesan, and season with salt and pepper. Toss spaghetti in pan so it's coated with all the ingredients and serve immediately.

SERVES 4

400 g dried spaghetti
small handful fresh
breadcrumbs
6-8 tablespoons extra
virgin olive oil
3-6 cloves garlic,
finely chopped
1-2 red chillies, seeded and
finely chopped
3 anchovy fillets, chopped
1 bunch flat-leaf parsley,
stalks finely chopped
and leaves roughly
chopped
small handful grated
parmesan
sea salt and freshly ground
black pepper

This accessible dish really is a platform to showcase olive oil. So many variations are possible — leave out the breadcrumbs and add a drained tin of tuna, or use different herbs in season.

Maggie Beer's
Broad beans with pasta and prosciutto

2 kg fresh young broad
 beans, shelled
½ cup extra virgin olive
 oil, plus extra for frying
sea salt
250 g fresh pasta sheets,
 cut into 6 cm × 4 cm
 pieces
1½ cups coarse
 breadcrumbs
150 g prosciutto, cut into
 strips
freshly ground black
 pepper
½ cup chopped mint
1 tablespoon red-wine
 vinegar

Bring a large saucepan of salted water to the boil in readiness for the pasta.

Add beans to another saucepan with just enough water to cover them, a dash of oil and a pinch of salt and simmer until just cooked - about 7-10 minutes. While beans are simmering, cook pasta in boiling water for 2-3 minutes, then drain (do not refresh it, as this removes so much flavour). Put pasta on a plate or dish large enough to spread them out, drizzle with a little olive oil and allow to come to room temperature. (Spreading the pasta out and allowing it to cool down stops it from cooking any further, and the olive oil stops it from sticking.) Heat 2 tablespoons olive oil in a frying pan over a medium heat and fry breadcrumbs for 1-2 minutes, or until golden and crisp.

Drain beans immediately when cooked and return to pan. While they are still warm, stir in breadcrumbs, prosciutto and remaining olive oil. Add pasta, season with salt (if needed) and pepper, then add mint, more olive oil (if needed) and vinegar. Serve at room temperature.

SERVES 4

The broad beans for this recipe
are picked very young, so they
don't need peeling. For a change,
try adding grated pecorino
instead of the red-wine vinegar.

Kylie Kwong's
Organic buckwheat soba noodle salad

1 small carrot

1 small cucumber, cut in
   half lengthwise

1 teaspoon sea salt

1 cup organic brown rice
   vinegar

1/4 cup organic brown sugar

250 g buckwheat soba
   noodles

3 spring onion stems,
   trimmed and cut into a
   fine julienne

1/4 cup coriander leaves

1/4 cup mint leaves

1/4 cup dill, roughly chopped

1/2 cup finely shredded
   Savoy cabbage

2 teaspoons roasted
   sesame seeds

1 large red chilli,
   finely sliced

Dressing

1 tablespoon organic honey

1/4 cup organic tamari

1/4 cup organic brown rice
   vinegar

3 tablespoons extra virgin
   olive oil

Using a vegetable peeler, finely slice carrot and cucumber lengthwise into ribbons. Cut carrot into a fine julienne then place in a bowl with half the salt and mix well. Place cucumber in a separate bowl with remaining salt and mix well. Set cucumber and carrot aside for 1 hour.

Combine vinegar and sugar in a small heavy-based saucepan and stir over a high heat until sugar dissolves. Simmer uncovered over a high heat without stirring for about 10 minutes or until reduced and slightly syrupy. Set aside to cool. Drain cucumber and carrot, and using your hands, gently squeeze away any excess liquid. Place vegetables in cooled syrup to 'pickle' them lightly.

Cook soba noodles according to manufacturer's instructions, then set aside in a large bowl. Add combined pickled vegetables with all remaining ingredients. Mix thoroughly using your hands.

To make dressing, combine all ingredients in a small bowl. Pour dressing over noodles and combine. Arrange soba noodle salad on a large platter and serve.

SERVES 4 AS AN ENTRÉE OR AS PART OF A SHARED MEAL.

The lovely slippery texture of the noodles contrasts beautifully with the crunch of pickled vegetables and sesame seeds. This recipe proves that Asian-style dishes can be enhanced with olive oil.

Grilled polenta with sautéed mushrooms and taleggio

In autumn after a light rain, we often get local wild mushrooms. They are deliciously earthy when sautéed and spooned over wedges of grilled polenta.

Soak dried porcini mushrooms in boiling water for 20 minutes. Bring 1 litre of water to the boil in a large saucepan, reduce heat to medium, then, whisking continuously, add polenta in a thin, steady stream until well combined. Stir over a low heat for 20-25 minutes or until thick and smooth, then stir in butter and parmesan and season with salt and pepper.

Grease a 20 cm square cake tin, transfer polenta to it then smooth with a spoon to even out the surface. Cover with plastic film and refrigerate until firm.

Meanwhile, drain porcini, reserving strained soaking liquid. Heat olive oil in a large frying pan over a high heat, then add fresh and dried mushrooms, garlic, shallot and reserved porcini liquid and cook over a low heat for 15 minutes or until tender. Add lemon juice and rind and cook over a high heat for another 5 minutes or until pan juices reduce and become syrupy. Keep warm.

Turn polenta onto a chopping board and cut into 4 or 6 pieces, depending on whether you are serving it as a main course or entrée. Brush with extra virgin olive oil, then grill on a hot chargrill plate or barbecue on both sides until golden and warmed through.

Stir parsley and marjoram through mushroom mixture and season to taste. To serve, place polenta pieces on plates, top with taleggio and spoon over sautéed mushrooms. Serve immediately.

SERVES 4 AS A MAIN COURSE OR 6 AS AN ENTRÉE OR LIGHT MEAL

10 g dried porcini mushrooms
$\frac{1}{2}$ cup boiling water
150 g polenta
40 g butter
25 g grated parmesan
sea salt and freshly ground black pepper
$\frac{1}{2}$ cup extra virgin olive oil, plus extra for brushing
300 g field mushrooms, trimmed and thickly sliced
500 g Swiss brown mushrooms, trimmed
1 large clove garlic, finely chopped
1 golden shallot, finely chopped
juice of $\frac{1}{2}$ lemon
1 teaspoon finely grated lemon rind
$\frac{1}{4}$ cup finely chopped flat-leaf parsley
2 teaspoons finely chopped marjoram
6-8 thin slices taleggio

Seafood

Living in rural New South Wales means I don't have ready access to a wide range of fresh seafood. But when I do get hold of some, I like to cook it simply - a piece of fresh fish only needs to be quickly pan-fried or seared on the barbecue and accompanied with a squeeze of lemon juice, a drizzle of extra virgin olive oil, a leafy green salad and some good bread. If you have some homemade mayonnaise in the fridge, use it as a base for a tartare sauce (see page 108) that is light years away from the gluggy sweet stuff sold in tubes at the local fish and chip shop.

Whole fish can also be filled with aromatics - a few sprigs of basil, dill or fennel, a little chilli and some lemon - drizzled with a generous amount of olive oil, wrapped in foil, then roasted in a 180°C oven or a covered barbecue for 20-25 minutes, depending on the size of the fish. The following pages provide some fresh ideas.

Steven Snow's
Chargrilled cuttlefish with saffron mayonnaise

First make saffron mayonnaise. Place vinegar, mustard, egg yolks and saffron in a blender or food processor and process until combined. Then, with motor running, add oil in a gradual stream until mixture thickens into a mayonnaise. Scoop out mayonnaise into a serving bowl.

To make parsley oil, blanch parsley leaves in hot water, drain and dry well, then finely chop. Blend in a food processor with oil and sea salt to taste, then strain. (This oil keeps for 2 days.)

Clean cuttlefish. Discard tentacles, place hoods in a bowl, cover with olive oil and add garlic.

Bring a saucepan of water to the boil, add potatoes and cook until tender (about 15-20 minutes). Drain, halve lengthwise and keep warm.

Roast capsicum under a hot grill for 3 minutes or until blackened and blistered, then place in a plastic bag for 5 minutes to loosen skin. Remove seeds, then peel and slice capsicum thinly.

Heat a chargrill pan or barbecue and grill chorizo until coloured and heated through, then set aside.

Place cuttlefish hoods on grill, cook one side for 30 seconds, then turn and cook the other side for 30 seconds.

Divide potatoes and capsicum among 6 plates. Top each serving with 2 cuttlefish and add chorizo. Finish with a dollop of saffron mayonnaise, a drizzle of parsley oil and some parsley.

SERVES 6 AS AN ENTRÉE

12 cuttlefish
80 ml extra virgin olive oil
1 clove garlic, sliced
3 kipfler potatoes
1 red capsicum (pepper)
2 chorizo sausages, sliced
handful flat-leaf parsley leaves

Saffron mayonnaise

2 tablespoons white-wine vinegar
1 teaspoon Dijon mustard
2 egg yolks
pinch saffron threads, soaked in 2 tablespoons hot water
200 ml extra virgin olive oil

Parsley oil

1 bunch flat-leaf parsley, leaves picked
2 cups extra virgin olive oil
sea salt

Steven first tried this combination in Portugal. He has added his own twist with saffron mayonnaise.

Janni Kyritsis'
Barbecued snapper with celeriac and radish salad

6 × 350 g whole, plate-
    sized snapper, scaled
    and gutted
sea salt and freshly ground
    black pepper
1 teaspoon dried oregano
extra virgin olive oil for
    cooking, plus extra
    to serve
lemon juice and lemon
    halves to serve

Celeriac and radish salad
2 teaspoons white-wine
    vinegar
sea salt and freshly ground
    white pepper
1/2 cup extra virgin olive oil
6 large red radishes
2 celeriac, about
    400-500 g each
1/4 cup roughly chopped
    flat-leaf parsley

Heat a grill or barbecue until very hot. Score fish lightly. A few minutes before putting them on the barbecue or grill, sprinkle with salt, pepper and oregano. Rub some olive oil onto the fish and grill until cooked, turning halfway through cooking (the time will depend on the heat of the grill, but probably 5-6 minutes per side).

Meanwhile, for the salad, whisk together vinegar, some salt, white pepper and olive oil in a bowl to make dressing. Grate the radish. Peel and grate celeriac (this is best done using a Japanese mandolin or other vegetable-slicing gadget). Combine celeriac with radish, parsley and dressing in a mixing bowl.

Put fish whole on serving plates. Squeeze a little lemon juice over the fish, then drizzle over some olive oil. Arrange salad around fish and sprinkle some extra salt flakes, black pepper and olive oil on top. Serve with lemon halves.

NOTE: It's important to grate the celeriac and radish at the last minute and to dress them as soon as they're grated, so they remain crisp and don't discolour.

SERVES 6

The Greeks like to put a lot of olive oil over their grilled fish, really saturating it, along with a good squeeze of lemon, which helps keep the fish moist as well as adding flavour.

extra virgin olive oil for
    cooking (about 250 ml)
2 cloves garlic, crushed
3 sprigs thyme
4 × 160 g salmon fillets
sea salt and freshly ground
    black pepper
1 bunch asparagus

Spinach purée
1 tablespoon extra virgin
    olive oil
250 g baby spinach
1 clove garlic, finely
    chopped
2 teaspoons grated ginger
50 ml cream

Orange sauce
2 golden shallots,
    finely sliced
100 ml verjuice
juice and grated rind of
    3 oranges
100 g unsalted butter,
    chopped
shiso leaves (optional)
dill sprigs

Janet Jeffs' Olive oil-poached salmon with spinach purée and orange sauce

To make spinach purée, heat olive oil in a saucepan over a high heat, add spinach, garlic and ginger and sauté until spinach has just wilted. Stir in cream and remove from heat. In a food processor, blend until smooth. Season with salt and pepper to taste and set aside.

Place the olive oil, garlic and thyme in a saucepan large enough to accommodate fillets in one layer, and place over a low heat. Season salmon and carefully add it to the saucepan, making sure it is just submerged in the oil. Poach over a low heat for 15 minutes or until medium rare. Carefully remove from oil with a wide spatula and keep warm.

While salmon is cooking, prepare a bowl of iced water and bring a saucepan of water to the boil. Add a couple of pinches of salt and blanch asparagus for 30 seconds, then refresh in iced water.

To make orange sauce, sauté golden shallots in a little olive oil in a frying pan over a medium heat until tender. Deglaze with verjuice, then add orange juice and rind and simmer until reduced by half. Whisk in knobs of cold butter until the sauce coats the back of a spoon, making sure it does not boil or it will split. Place asparagus back in boiling water briefly to heat through.

To serve, place some spinach purée in the centre of a warmed plate and top with salmon and asparagus. Drizzle sauce over salmon and garnish with shiso, if using, and dill.

SERVES 4

This is a special dish; cooking the salmon in olive oil adds richness. Ensure the fish is cooked no more than medium rare, or it will become too dry.

good pinch saffron threads

1.5 litres hot chicken stock

60 ml extra virgin olive oil

2 onions, thinly sliced

5 cloves garlic, finely
   chopped

12 anchovy fillets, drained

4 fresh bay leaves

2 cups arborio rice

$\frac{1}{2}$ cup dry white wine

$1\frac{1}{4}$ cups tinned chopped
   tomatoes

12 black mussels, scrubbed
   and beards removed

400 g skinless firm white
   fish fillets (such as
   blue eye or kingfish),
   pin-boned and cut into
   bite-sized pieces

3 Moreton Bay or Balmain
   bugs, halved lengthwise
   and rinsed under
   cold water

6 small squid tubes,
   opened out and cut
   into 4

12 large green king prawns,
   peeled (tails intact)
   and cleaned

80 g pitted Kalamata
   olives, halved

$1\frac{1}{2}$ cups finely chopped
   flat-leaf parsley

Steven Snow's
Arroz de marisco
(Portuguese seafood risotto)

Add saffron to hot stock and leave to infuse for 20 minutes. Bring back to a simmer and keep hot for the risotto.

Heat olive oil over a medium heat in a large, heavy-based saucepan. Cook onion and garlic for 8 minutes, stirring occasionally, until onion is golden. Add anchovies and bay leaves and stir for 2 minutes or until anchovies break down. Add rice and stir until well coated. Add wine and stir for 30 seconds, then stir in chopped tomato. Reduce heat to low and keep at a simmer. Stirring continuously, add 5 cups of hot stock, a cupful at a time, waiting until rice almost absorbs each one before adding the next. The rice should still be slightly firm.

Add seafood and remaining cupful of stock. Cook, stirring occasionally, for a further 5 minutes or until mussels have opened and the other seafood is just cooked. Discard any mussels that do not open, as this indicates they are not fresh. Transfer to a serving dish, top with olives and parsley and serve.

SERVES 6

This rice is much 'wetter' than paella. It is great shared at Sunday lunch and has a wonderful affinity with wine.

Meat and fowl

Meat and vegetables form the basis of most dinners at the farm. A simple steak, chop or sausages with mash and a salad are a godsend, as I can prepare them almost blindfolded. The great thing about these meals is that they meet nutritional standards - I take pride in knowing that a meal satisfies daily vitamin and mineral requirements.

Beef

As a beef producer, I have a bias for red meat and know a good steak from a bad one. We'll start with grass-fed beef, because I know you wouldn't dream of buying beef from a feedlot where cattle are force-fed grain. The availability of large tracts of land is one of the reasons Australia produces the best grass-fed beef in the world. Cattle do not naturally eat grain. They are meant to roam fields and eat grass, not spend their lives in prison.

Make your butcher your best friend and demand grass-fed beef. While you're there, order grass-fed lamb, free-range pork and some chooks who've been allowed to wander rather than live in claustrophobic sheds. Don't be fooled by the claim 'Export quality'. The best meat is grown for the domestic market.

Beef has a strong flavour and you don't want to disguise it, but a good marinade (see pages 98-99) can provide a welcome variation. Put the meat into snap-lock bags while it's marinating - this takes up less room in the fridge than using a dish. I rub the marinade into the meat with my fingers to ensure it's thoroughly covered. If you're not marinating, rub salt and pepper all over the steak before cooking. Please, *please* don't cut the fat off. Fat adds flavour. Leave it on your plate if you must, but it's better to eat it for the vitamins.

Heat the barbecue. While a wood-fired one is best, a gas barbecue or griddle on the stove will do. Cook one side of the steak until it's nice and brown. Then turn it over, just once. Don't overcook it - about 2 minutes each side for medium-rare and 3 minutes for medium. Turn off the heat and put the steak on a plate to rest for a few moments (a good rule of thumb is to rest it for the same amount of time as you cooked it). In winter I put aluminium foil over the steak to keep it warm, but I don't bother in summer. Meat at room temperature tastes best. Thinly slice before serving with olive oil, herbs and vegetables. The beef is the star of this meal, with the accompaniments the chorus line.

Lamb

Eight years ago we had sizeable flocks of sheep tramping around our hills, leaving their characteristic horizontal trails.

From a distance the landscape eerily resembled the terraced rice paddies of Asia. But although I loved the excitement at shearing time, we retreated from wool production when the price collapsed. However, we still keep a flock of sheep that are free to wander the garden, despite their tendency to nibble roses. There are two reasons for the sheep: they're fun and their meat is delicious.

A leg of lamb, marinated with garlic and rosemary, then slowly cooked over wood coals in the Weber is our favourite; the resulting meat is sweet and smoky. Another favourite is to rub a boned lamb shoulder with garlic and salt, then slowly barbecue or roast it. Rest the meat before serving, slice and place it on a platter, crush fetta over the top, and add chopped mint and anoint it with olive oil. Or choose any type of chop and marinate it before grilling. Sometimes we slice the legs to make huge lamb steaks. This is real, old-fashioned country food.

Poultry

I only ever use free-range organic chickens, not just because they've led a better, healthier and more natural life, but because their flavour and texture is infinitely superior to their mass-produced counterparts. Luckily such organic birds are now readily available and are no longer a niche product.

While chicken needs to be cooked through for health reasons, it is at its most succulent and flavourful best if only just cooked, as it can tend towards dryness. This is why it responds so well to being marinated and cooked in olive oil, or drizzled with a generous lug after cooking.

When roasting a whole chicken I often scatter fresh-picked rosemary sprigs over the bird, placing the stems in the cavity. I give it a generous squeeze of lemon juice and place the lemon halves in the cavity, too, then splash over some extra virgin olive oil and season well. I roast it at 180-200°C for 1-2 hours, depending on the size of the bird. I like to rest it, covered loosely with foil, for at least 20 minutes before serving, with all the trimmings, as this helps it stay moist and juicy.

Kylie Kwong's
Roasted beef fillet with sweet and sour dressing

600 g organic beef fillet
(buy in one piece if
you can)
1 tablespoon sea salt
1/4 cup extra virgin olive oil

Dressing
2 tablespoons finely sliced
spring onions
2 tablespoons finely
diced ginger
2 tablespoons finely sliced
coriander stems
1 tablespoon organic
brown sugar
2 tablespoons organic
brown rice vinegar
2 tablespoons organic
shoyu or tamari
1/4 cup extra virgin olive oil

Preheat oven to 180°C. Combine all dressing ingredients in a bowl, mix thoroughly and set aside.

Season beef fillet with salt and olive oil. Heat a frying pan over a high heat until very hot and sear fillet for 3 minutes on either side. Place on a baking tray and roast for approximately 12 minutes (for a medium-rare result). Remove from oven, cover entire baking tray with foil and allow to rest away from the oven or stovetop for 15 minutes. Cut it into 1 cm thick slices and arrange on a platter.

To serve, pour dressing over beef. You can serve this dish at room temperature or cold.

SERVES 4 AS AN ENTRÉE OR 4-6 AS PART OF A SHARED MEAL

Good-quality beef fillet served rare is the perfect platform for this rich, complex dressing — the olive oil adds depth and softens the salty, sour Asian flavours.

Beef carpaccio

I'm not sufficiently carnivorous to love raw meat, but many people do. Mind you, calling it carpaccio adds a little class. Meat prepared this way – finely sliced and dressed with herbs and olive oil – is actually very flavourful. If you're brave enough to give it a go, your taste for it will develop.

Combine salt, pepper, paprika and garlic powder in a bowl and set aside.

Slice beef very finely, using a thin, sharp knife (an electric knife is perfect for this, if you have one). Don't freeze the beef first - even though this makes it easier to slice, it dulls its flavour and alters the texture. Flatten each slice between pieces of baking paper, using the flat side of a meat mallet.

Drizzle a large plate with a little olive oil and vinegar, then swirl, just to cover the plate. Top with a layer of beef slices, drizzle with more olive oil and vinegar, then sprinkle with spice mixture. Repeat the layering with beef, olive oil, vinegar and spice mixture. Cover with plastic film and allow meat to come to room temperature.

To serve, divide beef among 6 plates, scatter with rocket and parmesan, and accompany with grilled slices of ciabatta.

SERVES 6

1 teaspoon each sea salt, freshly ground black pepper, sweet paprika and garlic powder
600 g piece beef eye fillet, centre-cut
1 cup extra virgin olive oil
2 tablespoons aged balsamic vinegar
100 g wild rocket, washed and dried
shaved parmesan to serve

1 tablespoon ground cumin

1 tablespoon ground
   coriander

extra virgin olive oil for
   frying

3 stalks celery, finely diced

2 carrots, finely diced

2 onions, finely diced

6 cloves garlic, finely
   chopped

$\frac{1}{4}$ teaspoon ground turmeric

$\frac{1}{4}$ teaspoon ground ginger

$\frac{1}{4}$ teaspoon ground
   cinnamon

pinch saffron threads

1 boned lamb shoulder
   ($1\frac{1}{2}$-2 kg), meat cut
   into 6 cm pieces

2 × 400 g tins chopped
   tomatoes

2 bay leaves

2 sprigs thyme

2-3 litres chicken stock
   or water

2 tablespoons honey

2 tablespoons harissa
   (see page 132)

1 cup pitted green olives,
   cut in half

1 tablespoon julienned
   preserved lemon

sea salt and freshly ground
   black pepper

1 cup coriander leaves

1 cup flat-leaf parsley
   leaves

Cath Claringbold's
Lamb tagine with
preserved lemon and olives

Heat a non-stick frying pan over a medium heat, add ground cumin
and coriander and heat briefly, stirring constantly, until they give
off an aroma. Set aside to cool.

In a saucepan large enough to hold the lamb, heat a good splash
of olive oil, add vegetables and garlic and cook over a low heat for
15-20 minutes or until completely soft but not brown. Add spices,
increase heat to medium and stir for 2 minutes. Add lamb, tomatoes,
bay leaves, thyme and enough stock or water to cover the lamb.
Bring to the boil, skim the surface of fat, then reduce heat to low
and simmer very gently for 2 hours or until meat is very tender.

Skim fat from surface again, then add honey, harissa, olives
and preserved lemon. Season with salt and pepper and then transfer
to a tagine dish for serving.

Scatter coriander and parsley leaves generously over the top
and serve immediately with steamed couscous on the side.

SERVES 8

*This recipe combines succulent,
slow-cooked meat, fragrant
juices, harissa and the subtle
sweetness of honey, and is very
easy to prepare.*

Stefano Manfredi's
Barbecued quails, red onions and sage

6 whole quails

¹⁄₂ cup whole sage
    leaves

200 ml extra virgin
    olive oil

sea salt and freshly
    ground black pepper

8 small-medium red
    onions, cut in
    quarters

¹⁄₃ cup balsamic vinegar

With a small sharp knife, take legs off quails at thigh joint and cut off breasts. Place legs and breasts in a bowl with sage. Sprinkle over ¹⁄₂ cup olive oil and season well with salt and pepper. Mix thoroughly.

Place onion in a bowl, sprinkle with remaining olive oil and season with salt and pepper. Cook onions until soft but still intact on a hot grill plate or in a frying pan. Place them back in the bowl, sprinkle with balsamic vinegar and toss.

Finally, grill quail breasts and legs, skin-side down, until golden and cooked through, then toss with onions and serve.

SERVES 6

The quails and sage are a great flavour combination and the balsamic vinegar and extra virgin olive oil, mixed with the juices from the barbecued quails and onions, make a wonderful sauce.

5 thick slices stale
white bread, crusts
removed
50 g freshly grated
parmesan cheese
1 clove garlic, chopped
3 teaspoons chopped
thyme, plus extra
for rolling
finely grated rind
of 1 lemon
110 g plain flour
2 eggs
2 teaspoons Dijon
mustard
4 chicken breast fillets
100 g firm marinated
fetta, thinly sliced
extra virgin olive oil
for cooking
lemon juice
sea salt
thyme leaves and sprigs
and lemon wedges,
to garnish
tomato and olive salsa
(see page 85)

Belinda Jeffery's
Crunchy parmesan chicken
with tomato and olive salsa

Whizz bread in a food processor until it's reduced to coarse crumbs. Add parmesan, garlic, chopped thyme and lemon rind and whizz it all again until breadcrumbs are fine. Tip mixture into a large, shallow bowl.

Pour flour into a wide bowl. Whisk eggs and mustard together in a shallow bowl. Pat chicken dry and remove the little tenderloin strip on the underside of each fillet. Carefully cut a pocket in the thicker side of each fillet, making the opening fairly narrow but widening it out inside. (Be careful here not to cut right through or cheese will ooze out as it melts.) Roll fetta slices in chopped thyme and stuff each pocket with them. Press edges of pocket together to seal it as tightly as possible.

Arrange the bowls of flour, egg mixture, and parmesan and thyme breadcrumbs in front of you to form a production line. Dredge a fillet in flour, shaking off excess. Dip into egg mixture, then let any excess drip away. Squash it down into breadcrumb mixture, pressing crumbs on to make them stick. As each fillet is ready, sit it on an oven tray lined with baking paper. Chill fillets for at least 30 minutes, or up to 6 hours.

Heat a shallow layer of olive oil in a large frying pan over a low-medium heat. Cook fillets until deep golden brown and springy; about 5 minutes per side depending on size. Adjust the heat as you go to make sure the crust doesn't become too dark and burn before the chicken is cooked through.

Remove fillets and drain on paper towel. Sprinkle with a little lemon juice and salt. To serve, cut each fillet in half, prop up one half against the other, then spoon a little salsa around them and garnish with thyme sprigs and leaves and lemon wedges.

SERVES 4

This lovely bright dish bursts with sunny flavours. Serve it with the tomato and olive salsa on page 85 — it contrasts beautifully with the filling and crunchy crust.

Spatchcock escabèche

Escabèche-style dishes are Spanish in origin. The term refers to a method of cooking fish or poultry in a spiced vinegar or a mixture of vinegar and citrus juice, then marinating the cooked meat in this liquid overnight. It is usually served cold.

Heat ¼ cup of olive oil in a large frying pan and, working in batches, brown spatchcocks or chicken drumsticks over a low-medium heat for 20 minutes or until golden brown. Transfer to a large casserole dish. Add onion to the same pan and cook for 3 minutes or until golden, then add garlic, bay leaves, allspice berries, peppercorns, herbs, orange rind and paprika, and stir for 30 seconds or until fragrant.

Deglaze pan with 1 cup wine, then bring to the boil briefly. Pour resulting sauce over spatchcock, then add carrots, remaining oil and wine, vinegar, orange juice and 1 cup water. Season with salt and pepper and bring to the boil over a high heat.

Cook, covered, over a very low heat (use a simmer mat, if necessary) for 25 minutes or until tender, turning halfway during cooking.

Remove from heat and leave spatchcock to cool in the casserole dish to room temperature. Once cool, transfer spatchcock, carrots and onion to a bowl. Strain cooking liquid and pour over spatchcock, then refrigerate for at least 12 hours.

Bring spatchcock back to room temperature before serving, then transfer to a large plate along with carrots and onions, and drizzle with a little of the warmed cooking liquid. Serve with sourdough bread, a mixed leaf salad and mayonnaise.

SERVES 4 AS A MAIN COURSE OR 6 AS AN ENTRÉE OR LIGHT MEAL

1½ cups extra virgin olive oil

4 × 500 g spatchcocks *or* 12 chicken drumsticks

2 small red onions, thickly sliced

6 large cloves garlic, peeled

4 fresh bay leaves

6 allspice berries

12 black peppercorns

6 sprigs thyme

3 sprigs oregano

3 wide strips orange rind

2 teaspoons sweet paprika

2 cups dry white wine

1 bunch baby carrots, trimmed and scrubbed

1 cup white-wine vinegar

juice of 1 orange, strained

sea salt and freshly ground black pepper

Sweet things

My friends in Tuscany never use butter for baking. All their cakes and tarts are made with olive oil. I've been swapping butter for olive oil for years and I promise you, the result is every bit as delicious - just use three-quarters of a cup of olive oil for every 185 grams of butter when you bake. Olive oil complements sweet flavours surprisingly well, adding a more herbal, complex undertone to cakes, tarts and biscuits than does butter. It also gives a more moist result, creating an extravagantly lush texture.

Muffins

This is the first breakfast my daughter learnt to bake.

1 egg

1 cup milk

½ cup olive oil, plus extra
  for greasing

2 tablespoons honey

a cupful of chopped bananas,
  berries, sultanas or nuts
  in any combination that
  appeals to you

2 cups self-raising flour

Preheat oven to 180°C. Mix together egg, milk, olive oil, honey and fruit
and/or nuts. Put flour into a separate bowl, make a well in the centre,
then pour in liquid mixture and fold flour into it. Grease a 6-cup muffin
tray with olive oil and half-fill each cup with the mixture. Bake for
20 minutes or until a skewer inserted into the centre of a muffin
comes out clean.

MAKES 6

Rachel Grisewood's
Honey and olive oil cake
with macerated strawberries

Preheat the oven to 150°C. Grease a 20 cm cake tin with a little butter. Line the bottom with baking paper and grease it. Dust all over with flour, tipping out the excess.

In a small saucepan, melt honey with milk and olive oil and leave to cool.

Beat eggs and sugar together until thick and creamy (5-7 minutes in an electric mixer with a whisk attachment or twice as long if beating by hand), stir in vanilla and gently fold in flour and arrowroot. Pour into the cake tin and bake in the middle of the oven for 40-50 minutes until cake is golden, puffed up and shrinking from the sides. Cool in tin for 20 minutes and then turn out onto a wire rack.

To make macerated strawberries, heat sugar, water, rosewater and vanilla bean in a saucepan and boil for 5 minutes. Slice strawberries into a bowl, pour over hot syrup, and leave to cool.

Turn cake onto a serving plate. Whisk cream until thick. Drain strawberries and spoon juice over top of cake. Spread cream on top and spoon the strawberries over the cream.

SERVES 8

butter for greasing
flour for dusting
75 g thick honey
80 ml milk
$\frac{1}{4}$ cup extra virgin olive oil
4 × 55 g eggs
125 g castor sugar
1 teaspoon vanilla essence
125 g plain flour, sifted
40 g arrowroot
300 ml cream

Macerated strawberries
100 g raw sugar
200 ml water
$\frac{1}{4}$ cup rosewater
1 vanilla bean, cut in half
    lengthwise
1 punnet strawberries

This is a deliciously moist cake, made richer with the use of honey and olive oil. It's great for special occasions in the summertime — perfect with a pot of tea or a bottle of champagne.

Granola

I make this whenever I have high-quality oats. For breakfast I fill a dessert bowl with plain biodynamic yoghurt, grate an apple to one side, pile the granola next to it and drizzle honey over the lot if I want extra sweetness. It's a nice dessert, too.

Preheat oven to 180°C.

Heat a flameproof roasting pan over a high heat, then add honey and olive oil and stir until combined. Add oats, nuts and seeds and toss until well combined. Transfer to the oven and bake for 10 minutes or until golden brown.

Remove from oven and leave to cool, then store in an airtight container.

MAKES ABOUT 6 CUPS

½ cup honey
½ cup extra virgin olive oil
400 g rolled (porridge) oats
100 g mixed nuts and seeds
(I always use sesame seeds
and blanched almonds, but
pumpkin and sunflower
seeds are good too)

Philip Johnson's
Lemon and olive oil cake

3 egg yolks

550 g castor sugar

¾ cup extra virgin olive oil

2 cups milk

grated rind of 2 lemons

juice of 3 lemons

300 g self-raising flour

½ teaspoon bicarbonate
of soda

pinch sea salt

5 egg whites

icing sugar, for dusting
(optional)

Preheat oven to 170°C. Grease a 26 cm springform cake tin and line with baking paper.

In the bowl of an electric mixer, beat egg yolks and sugar until thick and pale. Whisk in olive oil, milk, lemon rind and lemon juice, mixing well to combine.

Sift together flour, bicarbonate of soda and salt. In a clean bowl, whisk egg whites until soft peaks form. Fold dry ingredients into egg yolk and sugar mixture, then fold in beaten egg whites.

Pour cake mixture into prepared tin. Cook for 1¼ hours or until a skewer comes out clean when inserted into centre of cake.

Dust cake with icing sugar, if using, and serve with crème fraîche or whipped cream. It's also great served with fruit - for example, oranges poached in caramel.

SERVES 10-12

This is such a simple, pure-flavoured cake with a lot of vitality. It may sink in the middle as it's so moist, but this won't affect the flavour.

Tony Bilson's
Olive oil ice-cream

2 cups milk

250 g crème fraîche

1 vanilla bean, split

5 egg yolks

150 g sugar

100 ml Catalan or other
fruity olive oil

Heat milk with crème fraîche and vanilla bean.

Beat egg yolks with the sugar until mixture is light and foamy. Slowly add hot milk to egg mixture, mixing constantly, then place over a low heat and continue to stir until mixture thickens enough to coat a spoon. Add olive oil and freeze in an ice-cream maker according to manufacturer's instructions.

NOTE: You will need an ice-cream maker for this recipe.

SERVES 6

This sounds unusual, but in fact the fruity flavours of olive oil are brought out by the other ingredients, and the rich, silky texture is exquisite. If you make ice-cream at home, you have to try this.

Maggie Beer's
Apple and olive oil cake

3 eggs, separated

125 g castor sugar

75 g plain flour

½ teaspoon baking powder

¼ cup extra virgin olive oil

icing sugar, for dusting
(optional)

Poached apples

250 g Granny Smith apples,
peeled, cored
and chopped

1 teaspoon extra virgin
olive oil

1 cup verjuice

1 tablespoon chopped
rosemary

First poach the apples. Place apples in a large saucepan, add the olive oil, verjuice and rosemary and cook until apples are soft. Drain apples, retaining ¼ cup of poaching liquid for the cake mixture. Place poached apples in a round 20 cm buttered baking dish, ready for the cake mixture.

Preheat oven to 180°C.

Beat egg yolks with half the sugar in a bowl until the mixture is pale and thick.

In a separate bowl whisk egg whites and remaining sugar until soft peaks form.

Sift flour and baking powder into egg yolk mixture. Add cooled poaching liquid and the olive oil and stir until well combined. Slowly fold in egg whites (a third at a time) until all of it is combined.

Pour cake mixture over apples and bake for 20-25 minutes. It rises a little like a soufflé and falls back down again. Serve directly from the baking dish, dusted with a little icing sugar, with some Jersey cream or similar rich, thick cream.

SERVES 4-6

Extra virgin olive oil adds lusciousness to this cake. In fact, the grassier the better, as the flavour of the oil is as much of a feature as the moistness it gives.

Olive oil biscotti

Biscotti are the easiest biscuits in the world to bake. I'm partial to them because of their shape. They satisfy my sense of casual style and, like muffins, endless variations are possible just by adding a pinch of a new ingredient. I use whatever wheat flour I have, and add chocolate and/or nuts and spices and a tad more olive oil if necessary to compensate for the addition of extra dry ingredients.

Preheat the oven to 180°C.

Mix dry ingredients in a bowl, then add oil, egg and lemon rind and juice, and stir with a spoon until a dough forms. Turn dough out onto a floured bench, then use a floured knife to cut it in half.

Quickly mould dough halves into two long logs; it shouldn't be handled too much as this affects the texture.

Bake logs on a baking tray lined with baking paper for 20 minutes or until firm. Remove from oven and cool for 5 minutes or until you can handle it easily. Using a serrated knife, cut slices from the loaf, on an angle, to the size you want, then place slices flat on the baking tray and return to oven for another 10-15 minutes or until golden. You can bake them on both sides, but I usually don't as this makes the biscuits very hard and I want to keep my teeth!

MAKES APPROXIMATELY 20 BISCOTTI

240 g spelt or other
    wheat flour
165 g castor sugar
$\frac{1}{2}$ teaspoon bicarbonate
    of soda
$\frac{1}{2}$ teaspoon baking powder
$\frac{1}{2}$ cup extra virgin olive oil
1 egg, lightly beaten
grated rind and juice
    of 1 lemon or lime

Tobie Puttock's
Chocolate and olive oil tart

300 g dark couverture
    chocolate, chopped
100 ml double cream
100 ml extra virgin olive oil
4 eggs
100 g castor sugar
1 tablespoon maple syrup
crème fraîche or double
    cream to serve

Pastry
300 g plain flour
200 g unsalted butter,
    chopped
3 large free-range egg yolks
60 g castor sugar
pinch salt
butter for greasing

To make pastry, pulse flour and butter in a food processor until it resembles coarse breadcrumbs, or use your hands to get the same effect. Add egg yolks, sugar and salt. Process or mix until they combine to form a smooth ball of pastry. Wrap the ball in plastic film and place in the fridge for at least 1 hour before using.

Lightly butter a 24 cm flan tin with a removable base. Grate pastry into tin using a cheese grater, then, using your fingertips, press pastry across base and up sides. Put pastry case in the fridge for 30 minutes.

Preheat oven to 180°C. Remove pastry case from fridge and line with baking paper or foil, then scatter with pastry weights or some dried chickpeas or lentils or some rice. The pastry should have enough weight on it to prevent it bubbling as it cooks. Place pastry case in the oven and bake for 20 minutes; once done, remove paper and weights and allow it to cool in the tin. Reduce oven temperature to 150°C.

Choose a bowl that will sit comfortably on top of a medium-sized saucepan. Half-fill saucepan with water and bring to a simmer. Place chocolate, cream and olive oil in the bowl, then place it on top of the saucepan and stir to combine. Once chocolate has melted, remove bowl from heat and set aside.

In a separate bowl, whisk eggs, sugar and maple syrup until thick and pale. Using a spatula, fold chocolate mixture into egg mixture.

Pour filling into pastry shell and bake for 40 minutes or until chocolate has set. Serve cold, with crème fraîche or double cream.

SERVES 10-12

The quality of the chocolate makes a great difference to this wonderfully rich tart — couverture chocolate is best.

About the chefs

Stephanie Alexander ran the award-winning Melbourne restaurant Stephanie's for 21 years and is the author of the bestselling *The Cook's Companion*.

Chef, writer and television presenter **Maggie Beer** is one of Australia's best-loved food personalities. She ran The Pheasant Farm in the Barossa Valley for many years.

Tony Bilson is regarded by many as the 'godfather of Australian cuisine', and his restaurants have been milestones in the advance of Australian gastronomy.

Cath Claringbold is renowned for her creativity, passion and unique style of cooking, taking inspiration from Moroccan and Middle Eastern food to create her own distinctive dishes.

A native-born Québécois, **Serge Dansereau** opened The Bathers' Pavilion on Balmoral Beach in Sydney in 1999. Serge is considered one of Australia's trendsetters and leading chefs.

Holly Davis co-founded Sydney's Iku Wholefood, and has been a pioneer in the organic and biodynamic food movement in Australia.

Rachel Grisewood is the founder of Manna from Heaven and The Sydney Biscuit Company.

Russell Jeavons' Willunga restaurant Russell's Pizza has been open since 1992 and specialises in fresh, wholesome food in an Australian backyard style.

Belinda Jeffery is an award-winning author, television presenter and cooking teacher, and ran the acclaimed Good Health Café in Sydney for many years.

Janet Jeffs is head chef of Ginger Catering and The Ginger Room at Parliament House in Canberra, which opened in 2004 and has received many awards.

Philip Johnson's Brisbane restaurant E'cco has gained a national profile since its inception and has been critically acclaimed in both the national and international press.

In 1987 **Janni Kyritsis** opened his first restaurant, the award-winning MG Garage in Sydney, which was awarded three chef's hats in its first year.

Kylie Kwong is a TV presenter and cookbook author, and the head chef and owner of Billy Kwong in Sydney's Surry Hills.

Greg Malouf has inspired a generation of young chefs and transformed the Melbourne restaurant scene with the flavours of his Middle Eastern heritage. He is the resident guest chef at Stones of the Yarra Valley and executive chef at Mo Mo.

Stefano Manfredi has owned and run restaurants since 1983 - most notably The Restaurant Manfredi 1983-96 and bel mondo 1996-2002 - and currently writes the 'Seasonal Cook' column in the Saturday edition of the *Sydney Morning Herald*.

Sean Moran is the head chef and owner of Sean's Panaroma in North Bondi, renowned for its exquisite flavours, fresh produce and spectacular views.

Damien Pignolet wanted to be a restaurateur from the age of four, and is co-owner and executive chef of Bistro Moncur at the Woollahra Hotel and its sister restaurant at the Bellevue Hotel - both in Sydney.

Tobie Puttock became head chef at Jamie Oliver's acclaimed Fifteen in London in 2001. In late 2006, he opened a Fifteen restaurant in Melbourne, where he is currently head chef.

Steven Snow is the owner and head chef of Fins, which relocated from Byron Bay to Salt at Kingscliff in September 2007.

Index

Acknowledgements

Thousands of years ago, lantern light came from olive oil. A thousand days ago this book, which had been burning in my imagination, began to glow when Lantern, our most luminous publisher, gave it its blessing. Thank you, Julie Gibbs, keeper of the flame.

Thank you, too, Ingrid Ohlsson, for helping light the way with calmness, and to photographer Simon Griffiths for working his magic in photography, the art of light itself. Jocelyn Hungerford's editing removed shadows from the text, and senior editor Meredith Rose gave friendship and wise counsel.

Jo Hunt created the initial design concept, which Megan Baker pulled together into an impressive whole. Kathleen Gandy tested the recipes, and stylist Fiona Hammond helped give the food photography its warm, inviting appeal.

Thank you to all the chefs who contributed recipes. To all the other Australian chefs who have shared the delights of Australian olive oil with me through the years, but are not included within these pages, I am in your debt. Thanks to Rosemary Stanton, who knows more than I ever will about fats and oils, for answering, with patience, my questions.

I must share the limelight with members of Australia's olive industry. For all your support and inspiration, thanks to Paul Miller, President of the Australian Olive Association, who's worked tirelessly for years to bring the industry together; chemist Rod Mailer for answering endless questions; Peter Olson, who watches over the tasting panels; Chuck L'Heureux, who sorts hundreds of olive oil samples for competitions; Richard Gawal, who's helped us all develop our palates; Michael Burr, the industry conscience; Margaret Chidgey, editor of the *Olive Press*; and Margaret Kirkby, Nelson Quinn, Andrew Burgess, Mark Kailis, Maggie Edmonds and all of the Hunter Valley olive industry team.

Knut Kammann from Lakeland Olives, Jayne Bentivoglio from Rylstone Olive Press, and Neil and Jane Seymour from Mt Zero Olives provided hospitality and allowed Simon to photograph their beautiful groves and harvest operations. These groves are managed without chemicals and the owners are part of a growing network keen to produce food on naturally developed soil.

Thanks also to Gino Russo, who introduced Aurora and me to Sicily's olive 'traditions'; Fiorenza Roncucci from Arezzo; Meryan McRobert and Kiwa Fisher from Kerv café; Jamie Gray, who helps tend our olive trees; Chris Butler, who showed me the groves of Tuscany and then came to Elmswood to prune ours; and to Yvonne Mitchell, Gavin Prescott and Joanne Taylor.

And finally, if it were not for the people who have asked me 'How do I use olive oil?' I'd never have written this book. So to each and every one of you, thank you for asking.

But the biggest thanks go to my husband Phillip Adams and daughter Aurora Adams who put up with me - with love and understanding - while I wrote this book.